study guide

TO BOONE/KURTZ

CONTEMPORARY MARKETING

study guide

TO BOONE/KURTZ

CONTEMPORARY MARKETING

STEPHEN K. KEISER
University of Delaware

ROBERT E. STEVENS
University of Southern Mississippi

LYNN J. LOUDENBACK
University of Nebraska

THE DRYDEN PRESS
Hinsdale, Illinois

Library of Congress Cataloging in Publication Data
Keiser, Stephen K
Study Guide to Contemporary marketing.
Complements Contemporary marketing, by L. E. Boone and D. L. Kurtz.
1. Marketing—Programmed instruction. I. Stevens, Robert E., joint author.
II. Loudenback, Lynn J., joint author. III. Boone, Louis E., Contemporary marketing. IV. Title.
HF5414.K43 658.8'007'7 73-17260

ISBN 0—03—010786—5
Printed in the United States of America
56789 006 9876543

how to use the study guide

This study guide is designed to improve your understanding of contemporary marketing thought and practices. The manual complements *Contemporary Marketing* by Louis E. Boone and David L. Kurtz. It is an integral part of a total teaching/learning package that also includes *Readings in Contemporary Marketing* by Eugene M. Johnson, Ray S. House, and Carl D. McDaniel, Jr.

Study Guide to Contemporary Marketing is divided into eight separate parts. The part headings and the related chapters in the parent text are indicated below.

PART HEADING		RELATED CHAPTER(S) IN CONTEMPORARY MARKETING
Part 1	The Marketing Process and Its Environment	Chapters 1, 2
Part 2	Information for Marketing Decision Making	Chapter 3
Part 3	The Marketplace and Buyer Planning	Chapters 4, 5
Part 4	Product Strategy	Chapters 6, 7
Part 5	Distribution Strategies	Chapters 8, 9, 10
Part 6	Promotional Strategy	Chapters 11, 12, 13
Part 7	Pricing Strategy	Chapters 14, 15
Part 8	Marketing and Society	Chapter 16

Each part of the *Study Guide* provides a complete learning unit for a specific topic. The first section of each part is a summary of the *Contemporary Marketing* material on a particular subject, such as product strategy or promotional strategy. This is followed by a programmed review of the material in the textbook. The student is advised to read the summary and then work through the programmed review, before attempting to complete any of the assignments or caselets at the end of each part.

Programmed reviews reinforce what the student has read previously. It is an excellent method of learning and retaining the various concepts and information presented in *Contemporary Marketing.*

The student should hold an index card or piece of paper over the *answer column* on the left hand side of the page. Then, as you read the various learning frames on the right hand side, you should write in what you believe are the correct answers for each blank space. Your responses can then be checked by referring to the column on the left. Correct answers appear *one frame down* on the left hand side of the page. In other words, the correct response for frame #2 appears to the left of frame #3. The correct answer to frame #12 is to the left of frame #13.

The third section of each part is entitled Assignments. Some of this material is discussion questions for classroom use. A large part of it presents various exercises that can be used to gain a greater understanding of the concepts and ideas presented in the textbook.

Finally, each part concludes with several brief caselets concerning marketing problems. The caselets are designed to be thought-provoking and informative. They can be quite useful in stimulating discussions about various topics.

Conscientious attention to this *Study Guide* will enhance the learning experience and improve one's understanding of *Contemporary Marketing.* It provides a means by which to broaden the educational exposure to a most dynamic field of business enterprise.

The authors of the *Study Guide* will appreciate any comments or suggestions that will serve to improve future editions of the volume.

Stephen K. Keiser

Robert E. Stevens

Lynn J. Loudenback

contents

cross reference guide

CHAPTER IN *CONTEMPORARY MARKETING*	STUDY GUIDE PROGRAMMED REVIEW FRAMES	ASSIGNMENTS	CASELETS	PART NUMBER
Chapter 1	1–31	1–5	1	One
Chapter 2	32–66	6–10	2–3	One
Chapter 3	All Frames	All Assignments	All Caselets	Two
Chapter 4	1–32	1–2	1–2	Three
Chapter 5	33–80	3–5	1	Three
Chapter 6	1–20	1–4	1–2	Four
Chapter 7	21–49	5–8	3–4	Four
Chapter 8	1–39	1–3	1–2	Five
Chapter 9	40–76	4–7	3	Five
Chapter 10	77–110	8–11	4–5	Five
Chapter 11	1–18	1–4	1–2	Six
Chapter 12	19–41	5–9	3–4	Six
Chapter 13	42–60	10–13	5–6	Six
Chapter 14	1–38	1–4	1–2	Seven
Chapter 15	39–74	5–8	3–4	Seven
Chapter 16	All Frames	All Assignments	All Caselets	Eight

[1] The *Cross Reference Guide* is designed to assist those students who prefer to complete the *Study Guide* on a chapter basis.

study guide

TO BOONE/KURTZ

CONTEMPORARY MARKETING

Part One

THE MARKETING PROCESS AND ITS ENVIRONMENT

The basic reason why institutions are allowed by society to exist is that they produce a want-satisfying product or service. The creation of a product or service with want-satisfying power or *utility* has four basic dimensions.

First, form utility is created by the production function of the business firm. The production process involves conversion of raw materials such as labor, minerals, or agricultural products into a physically different product with more want-satisfying capabilities.

The other three forms of utility are created by marketing. These want-satisfying capabilities—time, place, and ownership utility—are created by making available production-created form utility at the time the consumer wants to purchase (consume), at a location convenient for the consumer, and under the proper circumstances so that the title to the goods can be assigned, permanently or temporarily, to the consumer.

Although marketing can be defined as the creation of time, place, and ownership utility, other, more explicit definitions have been suggested. The modern definition of marketing would seem to require an inclusion of the purpose of marketing effort as well as a description of the process involved in marketing goods or services. The extension of the definition of marketing, proposed in the text, emphasizes that consumer targets are selected and analyzed *prior* to production and not after the goods have been produced.

The definition of marketing recommended in the text is:

Marketing is the provision and efficient distribution of goods and services for chosen consumer segments.

In addition to the recommended focusing on consumer segments prior to production, two other aspects of the above definition of marketing are noteworthy. The definition assumes that marketing effort makes an effective contribution toward the long-range goals of business firms and society. These goal-satisfying efforts of marketers are assumed to be in accordance with the ethics of the society within which they are carried out. Moreover, true marketing effort should be carried out in an efficient manner.

Marketing has not always received major emphasis from the management of business firms or other members of society. Previously, production was considered the predominant business function by management and others. In some cases the emphasis on production resulted in a view of production as the only creator of customer satisfaction with no consideration of the effect of nonphysical dimensions of products such as time and place availability.

The previous lack of concern for marketing shown by businessmen and theoreticians is not necessarily indicative of their lack of business sense. A more reasonable explanation is that their production-oriented philosophy and resultant behavior was quite in tune with their environment. From the beginning of the exchange process to the 1930s, business firms tended to experience a market situation of production shortages and relatively abundant consumer demand (this condition can be called a *seller's market*). As a result, it is not surprising that management directed its energies toward solving the problem of insufficient production with present resources. The assumption at that time was that sufficient demand would be available if only *production* could be raised to the level of demand.

Changes in the mass-production capabilities of firms and large increases in the number of competitors following World War II led to an emergence of concern for marketing activities. Increased concern with marketing led to the emergence of the marketing concept. The marketing concept, a change in the firm's view of its mission, is defined as *a company-wide consumer orientation with the objective of achieving long-run profits.* The basic idea suggested by this concept is that satisfaction of consumer desires is in the best interests of the firm that is trying to achieve long-run profits.

The marketing activities a manager uses in implementing whatever philosophy he adopts toward consumers and profit goals have been grouped into four strategy elements:

1. Product planning
2. Marketing channels
3. Promotional strategy
4. Pricing strategy.

The product-planning strategy consists of deciding what products to offer the consumer, including all the related aspects of the product offered, such as brand names, guarantees, and warranties. Marketing channel decisions involve the establishment and maintenance of a pathway for goods or services from producer to consumer. Promotional strategy decisions concern the various methods a firm uses to communicate with consumers about its goods and services. Promotional activities include personal selling, advertising, and sales promotion. Price strategy deals with establishing levels of prices for different types of customers such as wholesalers, retailers, and ultimate consumers.

The management decisions involved in each of the four basic strategy areas cannot be made in a vacuum. Market failure of a product such as the mousetrap marketed by Pioneer Tool and Die Company may be traced to too high a price for the product offered in the selected channels of distribution and with the promotional strategy used. Quite possibly a change in product, channels, or promotion may have made the desired price of $29.95 a profitable one. Conversely, a revision in price may have made the other elements of the marketing mix effective.

Marketing is a relevant subject because

1. Marketing costs account for approximately 50 percent of the purchase price of goods. Detailed study of these activities may lead to an understanding of these costs and recommendations for improvement in the performance of marketing activities.
2. Marketing provides many jobs in the United States economy. Not only have many marketing jobs been available in the past but the increased implementation of the marketing concept may result in more marketing jobs in the future.
3. It affords human beings the chance to make relevant contributions to individual business firms and society.

It seems best to study marketing from the perspective suggested by a combination of five approaches—*commodity*, *functional*, *institu-*

tional, *managerial*, and *systems*—used in the past. A combination of these approaches should help the student understand the interaction among all the marketing activities that must be planned and carried out in order to achieve the long-range goals of business firms, consumers, and society.

Environmental forces, largely uncontrollable by marketing managers, must be carefully considered when planning and executing the elements of the marketing mix. These forces are divided into four types: competitive, legal, economic, and societal. The competitive environment affects the ability of firms to operate and may severely sanction firms operating in a manner contradictory to public desire. The competitive environment has both domestic and international sectors.

The legal environment, probably the most formally codified of all environmental forces, consists of governmental legislation designed to promote a competitive environment or regulate specific marketing activities. One important aspect of the legal environment is that the legality of business actions is dependent upon the situation surrounding the actions.

One of the first federal laws aimed at maintaining a competitive environment was the *Sherman Antitrust Act* of 1890 which prohibited attempts to monopolize or restrain interstate trade. Later laws were passed in an effort to correct the deficiencies of this act. The *Clayton Act* (1914), passed twenty-four years after the Sherman Antitrust Act, was concerned with price discrimination, exclusive dealing agreements, tying contracts, interlocking boards of directors, and stock acquisitions that tend to substantially lessen competition. All of these specific practices had not been interpreted as violations of the Sherman Act.

The conditions under which price discrimination is legal were clarified in the *Robinson-Patman Act* (1936). Price discrimination is legal if (1) the products are of dissimilar *grade and quality*; (2) price discrimination occurs in a *good faith* effort to meet competition; and (3) price differences reflect differences in costs incurred in selling to different buyers. The interpretations of these three exemptions have resulted in misunderstanding the meanings of (1) like grade and quality, (2) good faith, (3) meeting competition, and (4) cost defense. The result of these uncertainties has been the avoidance by marketers of price competition.

Several acts passed after the Sherman Act legalized certain activities that the courts had considered illegal under the Sherman Act. For instance, the *Miller-Tydings Act* (1937) was passed to allow manufacturers to require dealers to charge suggested resale prices.

These retail price-fixing agreements are legal only if states have passed fair-trade laws. The trend in resale price maintenance is toward less use by manufacturers and the repeal of these state laws.

The Federal Trade Commission, a quasi-judicial agency, has been charged with enforcing the Clayton Act and the *FTC Act* (1914) which established it. The activities of the FTC have been prime examples of the shift in emphasis of the legal environment from *protection of competition* to *overseeing consumer welfare*. This emphasis is the result of enforcement of the *Wheeler-Lea Act* (1938) which prohibits unfair or deceptive acts or practices regardless of their impact upon competition. The FTC has also tried to expand its authority to require firms that deceive consumers to advertise their deception (corrective advertising).

Another quasi-judicial body, the Food and Drug Administration, was established in 1906. This body is charged with preventing the adulteration, misbranding, and mislabeling of goods and drugs. Its responsibilities were assigned by the *Pure Food and Drug Act* (1906), the *Food, Drug, and Cosmetic Act* (1938), and several labeling acts.

Recent legislation, such as the *Fair Packaging and Labeling Act*, (1966) has substantiated the trend toward consumer protection. Similarly, the *Truth-in-Lending Law* (1968) reflects the desire of society to make consumers more informed about annual interest rates. An important lesson learned from these consumer protection acts is that providing improved information does not guarantee that the information will be received or used by the consumer.

The economic environment includes changes in the total level of economic activity (as indicated by the level of gross national product). Economic environmental phases such as depressions, inflation, and prosperity are of vital importance to marketers. These various economic phases are important because of their effects on (1) the willingness of consumers to buy; (2) governmental policies concerning government expenditures, taxes, and interest rates; (3) the perceptions of consumers regarding changes in the marketing mix variables; and (4) the degree of substitutability between products. Continued increases in the standard of living of a society result in more substitution between products and more competition. This increased substitutability has helped bring about a buyer's market.

The social environment has resulted in changes in the methods of marketing goods and services. In addition, society's demand that business be concerned with the quality of life has broadened the social environment of marketing. It is now necessary to consider the impact of marketing on society as well as the demand of society for *social goods*. The nature of this societal environment must be considered regardless of the marketing executive's familiarity with the society within which he is licensed to operate.

The societal environment must be considered in terms of such dimensions as (1) lifestyle of members, (2) store patronage habits, (3) attitudes toward business and its responsibilities, and (4) desire for change.

PROGRAMMED REVIEW

Assume that you and another student have started an underground newspaper. The purpose of the paper is to serve as an independent source of campus and community news. You have hired a secretary to type news copy with a typewriter you have bought for the firm. This information about the newspaper serves as the basis for questions 1 through 4 below.

1. The process of changing the information you have collected into a finished product, a newspaper, is mainly the concern of the
   ( ) marketing function.
   (✓) production function.

production function

2. These production-change activities are mainly concerned with the creation of FORM utility.

form

3. If you hire someone to deliver the finished newspapers to your customers, instead of requiring them to pick up their papers at your office, you have created PLACE utility.

place

4. You are in charge of contacting potential customers. You talk to students to determine who wants or needs an independent newspaper and how much they are willing to pay. In addition, after a sale is made you assign the title of the paper to the student. This activity in which you are involved concerns the exchange of title and results in OWNERSHIP utility.

In review, goods must be produced in the desired form and marketed at the right time, place, and under desired title exchange conditions.

ownership

5. Marketing has the goal of utility creation but utility creation must be carried out
   ( ) in accordance with ethical business practices.
   ( ) to satisfy consumer segments selected *prior* to production.
   ( ) in as efficient a manner as possible.
   (✓) in accordance with all of the above considerations.

in accordance with all of the above considerations

6. A firm that first produces a product and then hunts for somebody on which to unload it is PRODUCTION oriented.

production

7. Marketing is defined as the provision and EFFICIENT distribution of goods and services for chosen consumer segments.

efficient

8. Efficient distribution according to ethical business practices, business firms, and society goals does not ensure a marketable product or adherence to the marketing concept. It is necessary to choose consumer targets or segments PRIOR to production.

prior

9. The modern definition of marketing presented in Question 7 above emphasizes a ______ orientation.

consumer

10. Marketing activity develops as society changes. Marketing first becomes evident as a society moves from a subsistence level to one of production surplus and exchange of this surplus. As a result, marketing cannot exist without a surplus and a willingness to trade. Marketing does not exist until a surplus exists and people are ______.

willing to trade it

11. The Great Depression signalled the ending of a seller's market (one with a shortage of supply) and the beginning of a ______ market (one with an abundance of goods and services).

buyer's

12. If there are more goods and services available than there is demand, a ______ is said to exist.

buyer's market

13. The situation described in Question 12 above is called a buyer's market because the scales are tipped in favor of the buyer. The buyer has his choice of sellers to patronize and therefore the seller must pay close attention to the needs and wants of the ______.

buyer or consumer

14. A seller who faces a seller's market will tend to be concerned with
( ) producing more goods and services.
( ) convincing consumers to buy his goods and services.
( ) hunting for new markets for his goods and services.

producing more goods and services

15. In other words, a seller's market tends to result in a firm being ______ oriented.

production

16. The marketing concept is the management philosophy that generally followed the production orientation of firms and the shift from a seller's market to a buyer's market. The marketing concept assumes a firm's goals are
(a) ______
(b) ______

(a) consumer satisfaction

(b) long-run profits

17. The goal of consumer satisfaction should
( ) be assigned to the marketing vice-president.
( ) be the concern of all members of the business firm.
( ) not be the concern of a firm's accountants.

be the concern of all members of the business firm

18. The marketing efforts of a firm consist of many types of activities, all related to providing the consumer with want-satisfying goods and services. These activities, which are planned and carried out, cover many marketing activities and are commonly called a marketing mix. A consumer-oriented firm should plan the marketing mix with regard to the ______________________.

selected consumer segment

19. The marketing mix consists of four strategy elements:

(a) ______________________

(b) ______________________

(c) ______________________

(d) ______________________

(a) product planning

(b) marketing channels

(c) promotion strategy

(d) pricing strategy

20. A firm must decide what products to offer to the consumer and how to brand them. This is an example of the ______________ element of the marketing mix.

product-planning

21. A firm's decision to sell its goods through either door-to-door salesmen or retail stores concerns setting the pathway for goods or services or setting the marketing mix element of ______________.

marketing channels

22. The decision to use television advertisements in preference to a direct mail campaign is the marketing mix element of ______________________.

promotion strategy

23. The decision to reduce the selling price of goods is part of the marketing mix element of ______________.

pricing strategy

24. The important thing to remember is that all elements of the marketing mix
( ) must be treated as separate decision areas that should not be coordinated within the firm.
( ) should be production-oriented.
( ) are not of equal importance, as promotional strategy is the only element that should be planned.
( ) must be planned in conjunction with each other.

must be planned in conjunction with each other

25. Marketing is important because of its relative contribution to society. One measure of this contribution is marketing costs. Marketing costs and production costs tend to be estimated as equal. As a result, ______________ ______________ of the price you pay for goods is to cover the cost of marketing activities.

50 percent

26. As a result of the relatively high average marketing cost of 50 percent of selling price, some marketing critics claim that marketing costs too much. Realistically, the highness or lowness of marketing cost cannot be evaluated without some type of measurement stick. Unfortunately, all the measurement sticks that would seem appropriate to measure the effectiveness of marketing are hard to quantify. For example, the standard of living we have obtained is high but hard to measure. In addition, whether the 50 percent average cost is the result of implementation of the marketing concept is difficult to determine because it is hard to measure ______________ ______________.

consumer satisfaction

27. The text gave two other reasons for the study of marketing. They are

(a) ______________

(b) ______________

(a) lucrative chance for employment

(b) opportunity to make a contribution to society

28. Five approaches usually used to study marketing are

(a) ______________

(b) ______________

(c) ______________

(d) ______________

(e) ______________

(a) commodity

(b) functional

(c) institutional

(d) managerial

(e) systems

29. For each of the statements presented below tell which approach to the study of marketing is suggested.
   (a) Attention is concentrated on wholesalers, retailers, banks, trucking firms, and other institutions in a marketing channel.
   ______________ approach
   (b) Emphasizes the top management decisions made in establishing a marketing mix.
   ______________ approach
   (c) Another approach to marketing emphasizes studying each of the different activities performed to move goods from producer to consumer.
   ______________ approach
   (d) Concerns development of an effective distribution system for different categories of goods and services.
   ______________ approach

(e) Regards marketing as a functional element of the firm and business system.

_____________________ approach

(a) institutional (b) managerial (c) functional (d) commodity (e) systems

30. The best approach to the study of marketing is _____________________

____

____

a combination of all five of the approaches

31. The aspects of the environment that affect marketing decisions include

(a) _____________________

(b) _____________________

(c) _____________________

(d) _____________________

(a) competitive (b) legal (c) economic (d) societal

32. The marketing manager should consider the environmental variables as
( ) unimportant.
( ) controllable.
( ) textbook theories that are not applicable to real practice.
( ) important but uncontrollable.
( ) worthy of consideration only after the marketing mix has been planned and implemented.

important but uncontrollable

33. The pervasiveness of the competitive environment makes it difficult to determine the specific marketing implications of this environment. However, one definite implication of this environment is that it approves or _____________________ a firm to enter the competitive system.

licenses

34. A firm that fails to satisfy the members of the competitive environment will probably
( ) be very profitable.
( ) evidence declining sales.
( ) receive adverse public opinion.
( ) fail.
( ) lose its license to operate.
( ) experience all of the above except "be very profitable."

experience all of the above except "be very profitable"

35. The interaction of the four types of environments can be exemplified by consideration of the actions of the public toward marketers who ignore their desires. For example, legislation may be instituted against a marketer who produces a product that is considered harmful. The resulting legislation will become part of the _____________________ environment.

legal

36. Similarly, consumers may be unable to buy a marketer's products as a result of unemployment during an economic depression. Consequently, the public environment may be influenced by the ________________ environment.

economic

37. The societal environment also interacts with the public environment. These interactions among the various environmental factors often result in difficulties when one tries to classify an environment as one of the four types. Thus, the four types of environmental variables are not exclusive but are only a way of clarifying these forces and their impact. Because of this overlap of environmental factors the marketer should

( ) ignore all these factors.

( ) consider the resultant environmental effects of his actions regardless of which of the four or combination of the four factors he influences.

( ) consider the impact of each environmental factor separately.

( ) consider only the legal environment since it is the only one that has any power to harm business.

consider the resultant environmental effects of his actions regardless of which of the four or combination of the four factors he influences

38. The legal environment consists of all laws that affect marketing behavior. The Sherman Antitrust Act is part of the ________________ ________ environment.

legal

39. If a manufacturer of beer attempts to run its competitors out of business so that it is the only seller of beer, the firm is attempting to monopolize the beer market. Since this action is in contradiction to a competitive marketing system, it violates one of the first federal laws that clearly stated as national policy the maintenance of a competitive marketing system. This law is the ________________ Act.

Sherman Antitrust

40. Magnavox requires its dealers to sign an agreement that prohibits them from dealing with any other manufacturer of the types of products sold by Magnavox. This agreement of exclusive dealing, covered by the Clayton Act, is

( ) illegal if the Federal Trade Commission finds out about it.

( ) illegal only if competitors object to it.

( ) legal if the dealers involved *voluntarily* sign the agreement.

( ) illegal if the effect of this agreement may be to substantially lessen competition or tend to create a monopoly.

illegal if the effect of this agreement may be to substantially lessen competition or tend to create a monopoly	41. Thus, the actions covered by the Clayton Act are illegal only if they ______________________ ______________________ ______________________
may substantially lessen competition or tend to create a monopoly	42. Other practices covered by the Clayton Act in addition to exclusive dealing are (a) ______________________ (b) ______________________ (c) ______________________ (d) ______________________
(a) price discrimination (b) tying contracts (c) interlocking directorates (d) mergers	43. It is important to remember that the meaning of the original Clayton Act passed in 1914 has been amended by subsequent legislation such as the Robinson-Patman Act of 1936 and the Celler-Kefauver Antimerger Act of 1950. As a result of the Clayton Act and subsequent amendments it is illegal if ( ) Standard Oil Company requires its dealers to buy its automobile tires and batteries in order to be allowed to buy its gasoline (tying contract). ( ) G. Heilman Brewing Company purchases the labels and channels of the Associated Brewing Company (asset acquisition). ( ) Borden Company sells the same quantity of goods of "like grade and quality" to A&P for a lower price than to Joe's Corner Grocery Store (price discrimination). ( ) Ford Motor Company requires its dealers to sell only Ford products (exclusive dealing). ( ) any of the above substantially lessens competition or tends to create a monopoly.
any of the above substantially lessens competition or tends to create a monopoly	44. It is important to understand that various laws have not been given exclusive jurisdiction over a particular practice. It is possible that the practices cited in question 43 above could be considered violations of acts other than the Clayton Act. These practices may result in illegal monopolies or restraints of trade and thus be violations of the ______________________ ______________________ In addition, these practices could be considered unfair methods of competition and therefore be violations of the ______________________ ______________________

Sherman Act

Federal Trade Commission Act

Wheeler-Lea Act

45. The Federal Trade Commission no longer has to show that a business practice causes injury to competition. This is a result of the passage of the ______________.

46. The purpose of the Robinson-Patman Act is to
( ) prevent price fixing.
( ) protect large competitors from small competitors.
( ) prohibit price discrimination not based on a cost differential.
( ) prevent price discrimination that harms consumers with low incomes.
( ) protect all consumers.
( ) allow fair-trade prices.

prohibit price discrimination not based on a cost differential

47. A seller who offers a lower price to one buyer but not to another may not be in violation of the Robinson-Patman Act if

(a) ______________

(b) ______________

(c) ______________

(a) the products are dissimilar with respect to grade and quality

(b) price discrimination occurs in an attempt to "meet competition"

(c) price discounts are justified by cost differentials

48. Practical problems have resulted when marketers have tried to use these different price discrimination defenses. In the case of *like grade and quality* the courts have generally overlooked intangible aspects of the product, such as brand, when interpreting this part of the act. The court interpretation of *like grade and quality* was evidenced in the ______________ case.

Borden

49. As a result of the Borden Case, it appears that the courts interpret *like grade and quality* to mean
( ) the products have the same brand on them.
( ) the products are purchased by the same consumers.
( ) the products have the same physical characteristics.
( ) the products are manufactured at the same time.
( ) the products are manufactured by the same producer.

the products have the same physical characteristics

50. Use of the good faith defense has presented problems because

____

____

no consistent definition of good faith pricing has been possible

51. The third possible justification of discriminatory prices is called the cost justification. This means that different buyers can be charged different prices if
( ) the buyers are not in competition.
( ) the buyers have different costs of operation.
( ) the costs of producing and/or distributing the goods to the different buyers differ.
( ) the buyers do not object.

the costs of producing and/or distributing the goods to the different buyers differ

52. If a firm charged with violating the Robinson-Patman Act wishes to use the cost defense, it will have to produce statements that show that the costs of producing and distributing to one buyer are less than to another buyer. The major problem encountered when these costs are submitted as evidence is

____

____

____

____

obtaining the agreement of lawyers, judges, and Federal Trade Commissioners with the cost allocation bases used by the firm

53. One obvious way to avoid price discrimination among different buyers is to force the seller to charge the same price to all buyers. Moreover, if all sellers can be forced to sell at the same price to all buyers, there will be no price discrimination among buyers. Enforced price uniformity was initiated during the 1930s when manufacturers were given the power to set the price charged by retailers. The laws that permitted this practice were called

____

____

fair-trade laws or resale price maintenance laws

54. Fair-trade laws permit manufacturers to
( ) refuse to deal with black consumers.
( ) refuse to sell at a price below cost.
( ) enter into price-fixing agreements with retailers selling their products.
( ) enter into price-fixing agreements with competitors.
( ) produce and market inferior goods.
( ) force consumers to keep products they bought during special sales.

enter into price-fixing agreements with retailers selling their products

55. One of the major controversies connected with fair-trade laws concerns the legality of the nonsigner clause that was included in the laws passed in some states. The basic meaning of the nonsigner clause is that

____

a retailer can be bound to charge the manufacturer's suggested retail price although he has not signed a formal agreement

56. The current status of fair trade is
( ) increasing numbers of states are passing fair-trade laws.
( ) large discount retailers are pushing for more fair-trade laws.
( ) a *federal* law requiring fair-trade prices on all items has just been enacted.
( ) more and more states are now adding nonsigner clauses to their fair-trade laws.
( ) manufacturers are working more actively than ever to enforce the fair-trade agreements their retailers have signed.
( ) fair trade is decreasing in importance as part of the legal environment.

fair trade is decreasing in importance as part of the legal environment

57. The direction of the legal environment seems to be shifting from protection of competition to protection of

____

consumers

58. Many acts have been passed that require the disclosure of different types of information on packages. One law that *does not* deal with package disclosure is
( ) Wool Product Labeling Act.
( ) Fur Product Labeling Act.
( ) Fair Packaging and Labeling Act.
( ) Flammable Fabrics Act.

Flammable Fabrics Act

59. It is important to distinguish between various stages of business cycles, for each stage has different implications for marketers. Furthermore, the implications of a given cycle are not the same for all marketers. The demand for some products, such as nonessential consumer goods, may react more violently than that for essential goods. The *four* stages of business cycles are

(a) ____

(b) ____

(c) ____

(d) ____

(a) recession
(b) depression
(c) recovery
(d) prosperity

60. To check your understanding of each stage of the business cycle, give the correct stage for each statement below.

_______________ (a) From 1970 to 1972 this stage resulted in reduced luxury expenditures and increased personal savings.

_______________ (b) Consumers would be most willing to buy in this stage of the business cycle.

_______________ (c) Consumers may refuse to buy regardless of more aggressive marketing effort when the business cycle hits the bottom.

_______________ (d) Consumers may become optimistic after leaving the bottom of the business cycle.

(a) recession
(b) prosperity
(c) depression
(d) recovery

61. We have discussed the part of the environment that approves business firms and their manner of operation (competitive environment), the segment of the environment that determines codified prescriptions of acceptable business behavior (legal environment), and the environment that is concerned with the impact of different stages of business cycles and inflation on buyer behavior (economic environment). The final part of the environment involves the responsibilities of business to the members of the society within which it operates and is formally titled the _______________ environment.

societal

62. Two major impacts of the societal environment become evident when one considers the values of societies. First, many of the socially oriented objectives are concerned with quality of life in addition to number of goods produced. It is easier to measure

( ) the quality of life affected by a firm.
( ) the amount of goods and services produced by a firm.

the amount of goods and services produced by a firm

63. It is especially difficult to measure the immediate effects of a firm's policies on the quality of a society's life. As a result, attainment of societal objectives may be easier to measure in the

( ) long run.
( ) short run.

long run

64. The other area of impact of the environment involves two geographical market areas—domestic and foreign. With regard to foreign markets, the important point to note is that each country has different social objectives and behavior. Failure to consider these differences may result in

( ) strained personal relations between managers from different countries.
( ) marketing the wrong color product.
( ) selling a product with an obnoxious brand name.
( ) marketing the product in the wrong form.
( ) all of the above.

all of the above

65. The major pitfall to be avoided when marketing in the domestic market stems from familiarity with the American market. This pitfall results from the assumption that the domestic social environment is _______________.

homogeneous

66. When one considers the domestic market, the societal environments for black and white consumers, male and female consumers, young and old consumers
( ) are the same.
( ) are the same now as they were twenty-five years ago.
( ) need to be considered separately.
( ) are not important.

need to be considered separately

ASSIGNMENTS

1. It is sometimes argued that marketing creates form utility as well as time, place, and possession utility. Using the two examples of mousetraps cited in the first chapter, explain how you think marketing can create form utility. Be sure that you are able to define form utility.
2. Not all firms have adopted the marketing concept. Do you agree? Why or why not?
3. (a) Interview five friends to find out how they define marketing. Try to include people of different ages and backgrounds such as teachers, parents, roommates, and businessmen.
   (b) Do these definitions that you have collected differ from that given in the text?
   (c) Based upon your knowledge of these people, try to explain why their definitions vary from the one suggested in the text.
   (d) Why has the definition of marketing changed through the years?
4. Develop a list of criteria you would recommend using to determine whether a firm has adopted the marketing concept. Where possible indicate how you would quantitatively measure each of these criteria. Rank these criteria by importance.
5. Which of the four elements of the marketing mix is most important? least important?
6. (a) Do you agree that marketing is crucial to *all* organizations in their relations with *all* publics (consciousness three)?
   (b) How is marketing crucial to a church? an educational institution? a political party?
7. Laws such as the Robinson-Patman Act have been passed to protect small retailers from large retailers. "The impact of these laws is more harmful to small retailers because they cannot afford legal counsel to find the loopholes in these laws."
   (a) Do you agree?
   (b) What should be done about it?
8. "The only reason laws have been passed is that businesses have ignored the desires of the public. Therefore, if businesses will respond to the public they will avoid the need for laws."
   Discuss.

9. Assume that Congress is considering the repeal of the Robinson-Patman Act. What factors would you recommend that Congress consider before rescinding this law?
10. Most products are affected by the environment. One product that has received strong environmental pressure is detergent. Try to find examples of the influence of each of the four different environments on the marketers of detergents. Use publications such as recent issues of the *Wall Street Journal* for your sources of information.

CASELETS

1. Brown-Forman Distillers Corporation[1]

Brown-Forman Distillers Corporation, whose major brands are Early Times and Old Forrester bourbons and Jack Daniels Whiskey, became increasingly aware of the declining market shares of Made in America Whiskey Blends and Bourbons (See Table 1).

Table 1
MARKET SHARE OF UNITED STATES LIQUOR SALES

MARKET SHARE OF UNITED STATES LIQUOR SALES		
LIQUOR	1954	1969
Made in America		
Whiskey Blends	42.6%	20.9%
Bourbons	27.7%	23.9%
Vodka	1.8%	11.2%
Scotch	6.5%	12.6%
Canadian Whiskey	4.9%	9.0%

The decline in the market share for the dark, strong whiskies and increase in the market share for the lighter liquors were recognized as an outgrowth of the changing drinking habits of United States consumers. The drinking habits had changed from the desire to drink alone or to get drunk in dark bars to the desire to drink socially. The increasing number of social drinkers generally came from the female and younger drinkers who desired not to taste or "feel" liquor in their drinks.

In an effort to capitalize on this trend, Brown-Forman Distillers started to poll consumers in regard to a dry, white whiskey that was aged in used rather than

[1] This case was based upon two *Wall Street Journal* articles: Frederick C. Klein, "How a New Product Was Brought to Market Only to Flop Miserably," *Wall Street Journal*, January 5, 1973, pp. 1, 10. Klein, "Putting a New Product on the Market is Costly, Complicated, and Risky," *Wall Street Journal*, February 18, 1971, pp. 1, 18. The case is an expanded discussion of the Frost 8/80 example in the textbook.

new kegs. Twenty-four hundred persons were shown full-color photographs of four possible kinds of new whiskies labelled "light," "clear," "separate," and "dry-white." These people were asked to rate the photos of these new whiskies and one "Canadian" whiskey on the basis of a wide number of criteria. The "dry-white" whiskey clearly outranked the four other types of whiskies. Top management thought it was especially notable that the "dry-white" whiskey ranked very high on the characteristic of uniqueness. It was assumed that consumers would be anxious to try it if they thought it was a unique whiskey. The best response to "dry-white" was received from affluent, well-educated, twenty-five to thirty-five-year-old, fun-oriented, party-going types of people.

Further research showed that the "dry-white" whiskey was perceived by consumers as an "upper-medium" priced brand. Consumer opinions were also used to select the name of Frost 8/80 for Brown-Forman's new "dry-white" whiskey.

Overall, the consumer image that Brown-Forman decided was desired was one of quality. The traditional round shape and high neck of the bottle were assumed to project the image of quality. A silver foil neck wrapping was added to reinforce the quality image.

After consumer acceptance of the concept of "dry-white" whiskey was established, Brown-Forman acquired a stock of light-colored whiskey and began taste tests. The favorable reaction of consumers to the taste tests convinced the management of Brown-Forman that it had a winner.

One other part of the marketing mix-promotion strategy had to be set before entering the market. This strategy, which included plastic display stands for distributors and a recipe booklet (using Frost 8/80) attached to the bottle, was set, as were other marketing-mix strategies, on the basis of the expressed preferences of consumers.

The final product, which was launched on the market in February 1971, was a result of two years of effort and the use of eight outside marketing research or packaging firms. The total costs incurred for the research effort and the first year of production were approximately $6 million (See Table 2).

Table 2
FROST 8/80 COSTS (FIRST YEAR)

ACTIVITY	COST (MILLIONS OF DOLLARS)
Marketing Research	.50
Salaries for Executives during development	.25
Advertising	2.0
Accounts Receivable	.5
Bottling and Production Equipment	.5
Inventory	2.0
TOTAL	5.75

Based upon expended costs, Mr. Brown, the executive vice-president, forecasted first-year sales of one hundred thousand cases and then one hundred fifty thousand cases and two hundred thousand cases for the second and third years, respectively. Two hundred thousand cases was considered annual break-even volume.

By January 1973 (twenty-three months later), Brown-Forman had sold a total of one hundred thousand cases of Frost 8/80.

QUESTIONS

1. Did Brown-Forman employ the marketing concept when adding this new product?
2. Was there too much emphasis on marketing research data or are consumers too fickle to carry out any meaningful market research?
3. What would you recommend Brown-Forman do with Frost 8/80?

2. Food and Drug Administration

The Federal Food and Drug Administration is charged with protecting consumers from products moved in interstate commerce that are adulterated (defective either in their ingredients or as a result of processing and packing), misbranded (having false or misleading labels or packaging), or illegally marketed (not federally approved for safety and efficacy as required by *law*). The FDA appears to have been limited in carrying out its responsibilities by its inability to legally require firms to provide access to their records in order to assist in identifying and locating products suspected or known to be defective. An example of a firm that refused to provide the FDA access to all of its records follows:

A manufacturer of a liquid drain opener refused to provide the FDA with shipping records that were needed to show whether the product was shipped in interstate commerce and therefore, whether the product was under the FDA's jurisdiction.

The FDA contended that the product violated the Federal Hazardous Substances Act because it did not have an adequate warning on the label. The FDA had received several complaints that the product had caused skin burns. One consumer complained that she had suffered serious facial scarring because the product exploded spontaneously when she poured it into her kitchen drain. Had she not been wearing glasses, she might have been permanently blinded. Despite these injuries, the firm refused to cooperate with the FDA.

The FDA district office attempted to locate a sample that had been shipped interstate by obtaining consignee names from a trucking company and by requesting another FDA district office to try to locate the product. This attempt was unsuccessful, and the FDA was unable to take action to remove the product from the market.[1]

QUESTIONS

1. What changes would you recommend in the FDA's authority and resources to prevent the reoccurrence of similar incidents?
2. Why do you think a firm would refuse access to its records?

---

[1] "Lack of Authority Limits Consumer Protection," Comptroller General's Report to the Congress on Food and Drug Administration, United States General Accounting Office, September 1972, p. 11.

3. Do you feel this problem of limited access to records would be critical enough to worry about from a public policy viewpoint?

3. Congressman Triden

Congressman Jesse Triden reviews the grocery tape his wife brings home from the grocery store each week. Recently, he became enraged when he discovered that the store had charged his wife $2.95 for a broom she had not purchased. He also found that his neighbor had been charged for a broom he had not purchased. Both incidents of charges for unpurchased goods took place in the same store on the same day.

When the store manager was confronted, he refunded the money and apologized for the clerk's oversight. The manager did point out, however, that a broom had been left sitting at the checkout counter by another customer and this was why the clerk had mischarged the customers.

Congressman Triden has become convinced that the consumer needs to be protected from the reoccurrence of such incidents. He is interested in discovering alternatives for providing this protection.

QUESTIONS

1. What alternatives do you feel are possible?
2. Which alternatives would you recommend? Why?

4. Miser Construction Company

Oscar Miser has been a builder of custom homes for the last thirty years. His business has been very profitable by appealing to the wealthy residents of the suburbs of Washington, D.C. The price range of his houses has been from $60,000 to $135,000.

Recently, his son Bill joined the firm after graduating from a large university. Bill majored in marketing and was most impressed by the role of environmental constraints in the marketing process. Shortly after joining the firm, young Miser realized that his father did not serve the needs of all consumers of housing nor did he have any experts to forecast changes in the environment. Bill felt that his father's failure to build houses for the poor living around Washington, D.C. exemplified his failure to consider environmental constraints. Therefore, Bill recommended that his father hire a sociologist, a lawyer, and an economist and assign them the duties of forecasting changes in the societal, legal, and economic environment. These *experts* will cost approximately $150,000 a year. The company's profits have been approximately $100,000 a year.

QUESTIONS

1. If you were Oscar Miser, how would you answer young Bill's charges of neglect of consideration of environmental factors?
2. If you were Oscar Miser, what would you tell Bill about his suggestion of hiring the environmental experts?

Part Two
INFORMATION FOR MARKETING DECISION MAKING

The major purpose of this part is to inform the student about the nature and importance of relatively timely, accurate, and pertinent information for marketing decision making. The student should know the different stages in the decision-making process and the types of information needed at each stage. Moreover, the student should learn to define marketing research and the various phases of the research process. Specific types of research studies—sales and cost analyses and sales forecasts—are discussed. The student should also be able to explain the organizational status of marketing research and the nature of marketing information systems upon completion of this part.

Although marketing research activities are generally considered narrower in scope than marketing information systems, there are a large number of different types of marketing research activities carried out by firms. The activities are not the same for each firm. A comparison of the marketing research activities of consumer goods and industrial goods firms (see Table 3–1 of the text) shows a divergence between these two broad categories of manufacturers. As indicated in the definition of marketing research, a firm's emphasis in marketing research depends upon the types of problems encountered by the firm. Marketing research is defined as "the systematic gathering, recording, and analyzing of data about problems relating to the marketing of goods and services."

Not only does marketing research vary in content and sophistication in different firms but it has shown remarkable change since its inception in 1911.

The generation of information for marketing research purposes should start with recognition and definition of the present or possibly future problem facing the marketing manager. It is very costly, in terms of time and money, to proceed to gather data without a clear definition of the problem. Unfortunately, the problem-definition process is very difficult and it is a hard process to understand. It is possible to indicate what should be investigated in problem formulation, for example, present company objectives, marketing mix strategies, competitive strategies, and the status of other environmental variables. However, the ability to differentiate relevant from irrelevant information depends upon the experience of the decision maker involved.

Systematic gathering, recording, and analyzing of data are necessary in the first stage of problem definition. Before the problem can be precisely defined, the area surrounding the problem must be understood and some possible causes of the problem considered. The process of "feeling out" the problem through information gathered from persons and records available *within the company* and *outside the company* is the concern of exploratory analysis. Factors examined during exploratory analysis include characteristics of market targets, company marketing mix, competitors' strategies, and other environmental forces.

One type of internal data is accounting data. These data may be subdivided to uncover reasons for substandard profit performance. Several approaches may be used to clarify the effect of various factors on the overall profit level. Sales and costs may be separated to give a clearer indication of cause of profit problems.

The total sales figure can be assigned to the various factors—salesmen, territories, customers, or products—that are felt to affect the sales. The actual amount contributed by each territory, salesman, or other variable can be evaluated based upon a preestablished sales quota. This process, a sales analysis, provides the problem-solver with an improved idea of the problem although it does not prove what caused the problem.

Moreover, the level of sales attained by a given salesman or territory is only a partial measure of its contribution to company goals. The costs incurred in reaching sales levels must also be considered. *Marketing cost analysis* involves reclassifying the expenses as categorized during the general accounting cycle into *marketing functional accounts.* These costs assigned to different types of marketing functions, such as selling and advertising, are then allocated to the products, customers, or territories being evaluated.

The diagnostic value of such analyses when coupled with sales analyses should be recognized.

The increased use of marketing information systems should result in recognition of the value of continuously providing accounting data in the manner desired for marketing sales and cost analysis. The extra cost incurred by performing the reallocations will be much less if done when the accounting data are originally classified rather than when the need for the data is recognized. In addition, the availability of such data may reduce the need for expensive corrective action.

Secondary data already in existence are generally a cheap and quick way to get a better feel for the problem area. In fact, the secondary data provided by government, trade associations, advertising agencies, or universities may be so timely, unbiased, and pertinent to the problem that they can be used to define and solve the problem. The solution of the problem by use of existent internal company data or external secondary data precludes the necessity of incurring expensive *original research.*

Original research should be preceded by the establishment of purpose of the research investigation and the research design. The research design is the plan of attack for conducting the research. It must be set prior to conducting the research to ensure that the results will prove useful. Several questions that the research design must answer are *how* will the data be collected; *from whom* will they be collected; *how* will the collected data be *edited*, *coded*, *tabulated*, *interpreted*, and *presented*; and *what* should be done to *follow-up* the research study.

Survey, observation, and controlled experiment are the three major answers to the question of how to collect the data. Observation is best for studies of overt behavior but is of limited usefulness for obtaining insight into the reasons for the behavior. Survey generally offers the opportunity to ask a respondent to explain his behavior. The willingness of the respondent to provide this information is generally greatest for personal *surveys* and least for telephone *surveys.* Another method of gathering primary data is the controlled experiment. This method offers the advantage of isolating the cause of various behaviors without depending on the observers or respondents for interpretations of their behavior. Due to the excessive cost in time and money and the control problems involved, few firms have used controlled experiments other than for *test marketing.*

The results of the studies must be analyzed with regard to the user of the information. Any information is relevant only if the parties for whom it is gathered consider it relevant. Failure to consider the needs and desires of information users will result in the disregard of the information by the potential users. The user must be convinced that the researcher is gathering needed information and that he desires to present it in a manner understandable to all parties.

One definite objective of some marketing research projects is to provide forecasts of sales for future periods. These sales forecasts are vital to the planning, implementing, and controlling of marketing decisions. These forecasts set the production, finance, inventory, and raw materials procurement requirements. Without a reasonable guesstimate of the firm's expected output for the period, the input requirements will be set over or under necessary levels.

Many methods have been developed to forecast sales. One basic question in forecasting concerns the level of abstraction at which forecasting is started. From the viewpoint of forecasts needed to plan total company activities, the commonly used approach of top-down seems appropriate. Importantly, the development of forecasts in the sequence of general economic level to industry sales to company and product sales leads to more detailed forecasts at each level.

Generally, the huge multitude of factors operating at the national economic level makes trend extension more accurate at this level than it would be for industry or company sales.

The technique of sales forecasting chosen depends upon the degree of accuracy a firm desires and how quickly the forecast is needed. In many cases, the cost to a firm of an inaccurate forecast would not cover the cost of obtaining a more accurate forecast.

All the types of information needed by a firm to make marketing decisions must be delineated and a systematic approach to gathering and disseminating this information must be established. A successful *marketing information system* does not just happen. It must be carefully planned and implemented so that information is available when needed. Unfortunately, many firms have allowed their information functions to be overly influenced by particular members of the firm. Consequently, the information may be received by the wrong person, at the wrong time, and in the wrong form.

A very important aspect to consider in the design of a marketing information system is the nature of the information needed by marketing decision makers. Adopters of marketing information systems must also be sure that top management supports the marketing information system effort and that the marketing information system fits into existent organizational structures.

PROGRAMMED REVIEW

1. Marketing research is a process with a purpose. The nature of this process is indicated by the American Marketing Association definition of marketing research. This process is ______________________________

____

____

the systematic gathering, recording, and analyzing of data

2. The purpose of marketing research is to
   ( ) replace marketing decision makers.
   ( ) provide more data than can be used by a firm's decision makers.
   ( ) provide relevant information so decision makers can make effective decisions.
   ( ) provide technological improvements in products.

provide relevant information so decision makers can make effective decisions

3. The exact nature of marketing research activities varies for different types of firms. In general, the three most common marketing research activities are
   ( ) sales forecasting.
   ( ) sales analyses.
   ( ) test markets.
   ( ) determining new product acceptance and potential.
   ( ) consumer panel operations.

sales forecasting

sales analyses

determining new product acceptance and potential (Table 3–1)

4. In general, the amount of research activities varies for consumer goods manufacturers, industrial goods manufacturers, and retailers and wholesalers. Frequently, research appears more necessary for the firms that have to design and produce the product and less necessary for those firms distributing these products. The fewest research activities are carried out by ________________ and ________________.

retailers

wholesalers (Table 3–1)

5. Major differences are also recognizable between consumer goods manufacturers and industrial goods manufacturers, as consumer goods manufacturers are more likely to perform research on consumers, advertising, and test markets. As compared to industrial goods manufacturers, the marketing research activities of consumer goods manufacturers are less likely to consist of
   ( ) studies of advertising effectiveness.
   ( ) packaging research design.
   ( ) test marketing.
   ( ) consumer panel operations.
   ( ) long-range forecasting.

long-range forecasting (Table 3–1)

6. The various stages of the decision-making process involve recognizing problems or opportunities and deciding what to do about these problems or opportunities. The actual making of decisions, the implementation of these decisions, and the evaluation of the outcomes of these decisions are also integral parts of the decision-making process. The first stage in the decision-making process is ________________

____

____

recognition of problems and opportunities (Figure 3–3)

7. The types of information needed for various stages of the decision-making process vary. During the first stage of the decision-making process, information is needed to help management recognize problems and opportunities. To determine if actual performance is bad, performance standards must be set. Similarly, information is needed about new opportunities. In the problem and opportunity-recognition stage, past sales data can be used to set ________________

____

____

____

performance standards

indicate changed conditions or new opportunities (Figure 3–3)

8. In the problem-definition stage, information about causes of the problem is needed. It is necessary to find out what factors affect ________________

____

performance (Figure 3–3)

9. Past sales figures can be used to determine what caused performance to be below expectations. The total sales figure must be broken down so that the sales contributed by salesmen, territories, or other factors can be evaluated. This breakdown of sales into components in order to find the cause of the problem is a ________________

____

sales analysis

10. Past sales data may also be used in the decision-making stage of the management process. The information is used to ________________ ________________ of alternative causes of action.

predict results

11. After a decision has been made, the decision must be implemented and controlled. The purpose of research information gathered for control purposes is to ________________

____

measure performance (Figure 3–3)

12. The marketing research process starts with a task that is a stage in all management decision making. Assuming that the research investigation starts after the problem or opportunity is noticed, the first thing to do is to

____

define the problem or opportunity

13. The process of problem definition is a ______________________ of the researcher.

task

14. The problem-definition process is difficult to delineate. One common pitfall encountered in the problem-definition stage is confusion of *symptoms* and *problems.* A symptom is a sign of an occurrence. In general, if the nature of this occurrence does not meet expectations, a ______________ ______________ of something being wrong is noted.

symptom

15. If a firm's sales are lower than expected, the low sales would be considered a ______________________.

symptom

16. The problem is concerned with the *underlying reason* for the occurrence. The problem is defined as ____
____
____

the reason for occurrence of the symptom

17. Therefore, the researcher defines the problem facing a firm with substandard earnings to be ____
____
____

whatever caused the substandard sales

18. In order to define the problem, a marketing researcher must gather data about the company, its strategies, and the environment within which it operates. The purpose of these data is to explore the problem areas in order to gain ______________________ into the causes and effects of the problem. This preliminary data-gathering is called ______________ ______________ research.

insight

exploratory

19. The purpose of exploratory research is to give the researcher ______________
____
____

an understanding of the problem and its causes and effects

20. During an exploratory investigation, data may be gathered from internal company sources or external sources such as United States Government reports or ______________________ organizations.

private

21. During an exploratory investigation a researcher may
( ) discuss the problem area with salesmen.
( ) conduct a sales analysis.

( ) determine the nature of the objectives of the company.
( ) read the results of the United States Census of Population.
( ) purchase consumer panel data gathered by Market Research Corporation of America (MRCA).
( ) do any of the above.

do any of the above

22. Sources of data available within a company vary depending upon the firm and the degree of sophistication of its marketing information system. These *internal* data should be investigated prior to consideration of external data because ______________________________

____

____

they are easier to obtain and generally less expensive

23. If information is desired quickly and with minimal expense, the researcher should examine ______________ data.

internal

24. Data collected by the United States Government would be available outside the company. This is an example of ______________ data.

external

25. Accounting data are one type of internal data. Generally, accounting data have not been prepared in terms of the factors that can affect the performance of the firm. The general sales and cost data provided by accounting are of limited use for determining causes of problems because
( ) they are unreliable.
( ) they are not detailed enough in breakdown.
( ) cost data are not reported.

they are not detailed enough in breakdown

26. Sales and cost analyses are two processes involved in further breakdown of accounting data. The bases upon which sales or costs can be broken down are anything considered to affect the sales or cost performance of a firm. Possible bases for breakdowns are

(a) ______________________________

(b) ______________________________

(c) ______________________________

(d) ______________________________

(e) ______________________________

(a) sales territories
(b) salesmen
(c) products
(d) types of customers
(e) order sizes

27. The general procedure for conducting a sales analysis is the same as that used in a cost analysis. The actual sales are allocated to the territories, salesmen, and so on and then compared to ________________ ________________ for the chosen marketing factors.

expected sales

28. The purpose of sales and cost analyses is to determine the specific problem area. However, further analysis is necessary to determine the cause of the problem. Thus, after the completion of a sales or cost analysis the decision maker should try to determine the ________________ of the problem.

cause

29. If actual sales for a territory are lower than *expected*, then
( ) the characteristics of the territory should be specifically investigated in order to determine why the quota was not met.
( ) the territory should be dropped.
( ) more promotional dollars should be allocated to the territory.
( ) the quota for the teritory should be lowered.

the characteristics of the territory should be specifically investigated in order to determine why the quota was not met

30. The failure of a territory to meet expected sales may be offset if the marketing costs of the territory are lower than expected. In order to assess the profitability of sales territories or other marketing factors both a ________________ analysis and a ________________ ________________ analysis should be carried out.

sales
cost

31. A marketing ________________ analysis requires a new way of classifying accounting data. Many of the accounts traditionally used by accountants do not refer specifically to one type of marketing activity or function. Therefore, the traditional ________________ accounts must be reallocated to ________________ accounts or the purpose for which expenditure was made.

cost
natural
functional

32. Secondary data are data gathered and reported for a purpose other than those currently being considered by the marketing researcher. Despite time lags and differences in research purposes, secondary data should be considered prior to collection of original or primary data. Secondary data are preferred over primary data because they are less ________________ ________________ and take ________________ time to collect.

expensive less	33. To demonstrate the limitations of secondary data, assume that you are currently concerned with potential sales of waterbeds in the state of Illinois. The only secondary data you can find is a report on the total dollar waterbed sales for the three states of Illinois, Indiana, and Ohio. The study, performed by the Conventional Bed Manufacturers Association, was done in 1955. Inherent problems with using these secondary data are (a) the data may be ________. (b) the ________ of the data may not be usable in the study. (c) the collector of the data may be ________.
(a) obsolete (b) classification (c) biased	34. If secondary data do not provide the desired information, the only alternative is ________ data.
primary	35. Prior to gathering ________ data, a model for conducting the research must be set or designed. This master plan is the ________.
primary research design	36. The researcher has three alternatives for gathering primary data. They are (a) ________ (b) ________ (c) ________
(a) survey (b) observation (c) controlled experiment	37. If the data desired are information about the overt behavior of shoppers in a supermarket, the method most likely used is ________.
observation	38. If the researcher were to *ask* consumers about their behavior, a ________ would be employed.
survey	39. If you wanted to survey people to find out if they had ever heard of your brand of product and you wanted to gather the data from one thousand people in two days, the type of survey used would probably be ( ) personal. ( ) telephone. ( ) mail.

telephone

40. The advantages of a telephone survey are

(a) ____________________

(b) ____________________

(a) speed

(b) inexpensive

41. ____________________ interviews allow the marketing researcher to conduct national studies at ____________________ costs. However, the idea of a fixed cost for each questionnaire mailed is misleading. Mail interviews may be costly as only ____________________ percent of those receiving questionnaires may return them.

mail

reasonable

10–20

42. The major problem with a low mail response rate is not the increased costs. The biases that result from the nonrespondents are very dangerous. There may be ____________________ differences between the characteristics of respondents and ____________________.

important

nonrespondents

43. In addition to mail and telephone surveys, survey data can be gathered by ____________________. The advantage of personal interviews is that the interviewer may explain questions to respondents. Even though personal interviews are flexible, they are also a ____________________ and ____________________ method of gathering survey data.

personal interview

slow

expensive

44. Generally, surveys or observations do not enable marketers to determine what caused the behavior that has been measured. In order to determine the cause of behavior, one variable should be changed while all other variables are controlled. This method of information collection is ____________________.

controlled experiments

45. Another decision in the primary research process concerns the selection of the people to be observed, surveyed, or experimented with. Because of costs, all possible people are not questioned; instead a smaller group or ____________________ is chosen.

sample

46. The major criterion used when selecting the members of the sample is that the group sampled be representative of the population. One way to select a sample with a high probability of being representative is to make sure each member of the population has an equal chance of being selected for the sample. Another name for this equal-chance selection method is ____________________ sampling.

simple random

47. Many excellent research reports are ignored by the managers who requested the information. In order to reduce the likelihood of rejection of research reports, many factors must be considered. One of the major factors is to make sure the researcher understands the needs, desires, and characteristics

of the potential *users of the information.* Therefore, the *caveat* to the researcher is to know the ______________________________

____

user of the information

48. The user of the research report must be considered when ______________ ______________ the final report.

preparing

49. Frequently, decision making is concerned with planning for future production, financial needs, inventory levels, personnel, and other procurement needs. One vital form of marketing information needed to plan for these needs concerns the ______________ of goods from the firm. ______________ are measurements of this outflow of goods. The process of estimating company sales for a specified future period is defined as ______________.

output

sales

sales forecasting

50. Forecasts can be made for many levels of economic activity ranging from the total economy level to the industry and company levels. Methods used to forecast these various levels may change, although there are no universally accepted forecasting methods for a particular level of activity. One method frequently used to extend GNP—an indicator of the level of economic activity—is to base the future on past trends. This trend extension is very appealing because of its ______________.

simplicity

51. To show the shortcoming of trend extension, assume that you find that the average rate of increase in GNP in the last ten years has been 10 percent yearly and the current year's GNP is 1 billion dollars. Based upon a 10 percent annual rate of growth, you would project $ ______________ ______________ billion as the level of GNP for next year.

$1.1

52. If the United States government suddenly cut its military expenditures by 90 percent, the impact on GNP might result in a substantial variation from the average 10 percent growth. As a result, trend extension has the shortcoming that it implicitly assumes that ______________

____

____

____

those factors that contributed to the attainment of a certain level of output in the past will continue to operate in the same manner in the future

53. Marketing research has had a relatively short history, as its origin is traced to the year ______________.

1911

54. Relatively speaking, the concept of marketing information systems is ________________ older/younger than marketing research.

younger (originated 1961)

55. The relative age of the two concepts—marketing research and marketing information systems—can be highlighted by a comparison of the proportion of firms possessing formal research departments and an operational marketing information system. ________________ percent of the firms responding possess formal marketing research departments while ________________ percent of responding firms possess an operational marketing information system.

82

39

56. The marketing information system (MIS) is a *designed set of procedures and methods for generating an orderly flow of pertinent information for use in making decisions, providing management with the current and future status of the market, and also providing indications of market responses to company actions as well as the actions of competitors.* The purpose of an MIS is to ________________ an ________________ ________________ of ________________ data for ________________ making.

generate an orderly flow

pertinent

decision

57. Better understanding of the nature of the MIS results if the process involved in the design of an MIS is considered. The first step in the process is to obtain ________________ support.

top management

58. Top management support may be difficult to get because top management may not feel the company needs an MIS. Two frequently stated reasons for this feeling of lack of need are that
(a) the company is too ________________.
(b) marketing research ________________ needed.

(a) small

(b) supplies information

59. The manager who retorts that no MIS is needed because a marketing research department is already in existence misunderstands the concept of MIS. The major advantages of marketing information systems over marketing research are
(a) the MIS involves ________________ collection of information and
(b) the MIS involves ________________ of all information-gathering efforts of the firm.

(a) continuous

(b) coordination

60. Once top management support of the MIS has been gained, the next step involves an exploratory analysis of the entire marketing organization within which the MIS will operate. The purpose of this stage is to define the marketing manager's ________________.

responsibilities

61. The third stage of the MIS design process concerns the actual determination of the nature or level of sophistication of the MIS. The level of sophistication of the system should depend upon

( ) the costs incurred in gathering information.
( ) the information decision makers feel they need to carry out their responsibilities.
( ) the ability of the managers to understand the information.
( ) all of the above.

all of the above

62. After the system has been designed, it is implemented and ______________ ______________ to determine the ______________ of the MIS.

monitored

success

ASSIGNMENTS

1. How do the research activities of consumer goods manufacturers differ from those of wholesalers and retailers? Why?
2. Why is it necessary to carry out both a sales and cost analysis?
3. A group of minority businessmen joined together in order to market a new perfume called "Musk Oil." They decided to test market it in Peoria, Illinois prior to launching national distribution. After three months of testing the "Musk Oil," they had a 2 percent share of all the perfume sales. Is this a controlled experiment? Why or why not?
4. You have been hired by a firm to evaluate its marketing information system. How would you carry out this job? Explain the nature of and reason for each step you would take.
5. What factors should be considered when deciding how many people should be sampled?

CASELETS

1. The Pensol Company

The Pensol Company has performed a sales and cost analysis in order to determine why its total sales have dropped from $100,000 in 1971 to $80,000 in 1972. The company has three salesmen—Ames, Block, and Car—who call upon customers and try to influence them to buy one of the three products sold by the Pensol Company. The three products are electric sanders, electric drills, and electric saws.

Table 1
SALESMEN'S PERFORMANCE (1971–1972)

	AMES		BLOCK		CAR		TOTAL	
	1971	1972	1971	1972	1971	1972	1971	1972
Sales	$50,000	$58,000	$30,000	$10,000	$20,000	$12,000	$100,000	$80,000
Cost of Sales	30,000	46,000	18,000	6,000	12,000	6,000	60,000	58,000
Gross Margin	$20,000	$12,000	$12,000	$ 4,000	$ 8,000	$ 6,000	$ 40,000	$22,000
Marketing Expenses	14,000	10,000	10,000	1,000	6,000	1,000	30,000	12,000
Contribution of Each Salesman	$ 6,000	$ 2,000	$ 2,000	$ 3,000	$ 2,000	$ 5,000	$ 10,000	$10,000

Table 2
PRODUCT SALES FOR EACH SALESMAN

	AMES		BLOCK		CAR		TOTAL	
	1971	1972	1971	1972	1971	1972	1971	1972
Drills	$15,000	$25,000	$ 5,000	$ 5,000	$ 5,000	$ 5,000	$ 25,000	$35,000
Sanders	10,000	30,000	15,000	4,000	0	6,000	25,000	40,000
Saws	25,000	3,000	10,000	1,000	15,000	1,000	50,000	5,000
TOTAL	$50,000	$58,000	$30,000	$10,000	$20,000	$12,000	$100,000	$80,000

A sales and cost analysis of the three salesmen resulted in the information shown in Table 1.

Product sales are shown for each salesman in Table 2.

QUESTIONS

1. What problems are facing the Pensol Company?
2. What other information, if any, would you need prior to suggesting action to correct the problems?

2. The BoClog Company

The BoClog Company is introducing a new line of shoes that are a combination of the open-heeled clog and the knee-high boot. Management is very enthusiastic about the profit potential of the product which they plan to sell in bars located in university towns.

In an effort to determine the potential of these new shoes, bar owners and bartenders were polled concerning this new product. These bar owners and bartenders indicated they could sell one million pairs of BoClogs the first year. Management had previously estimated that sales of eight hundred thousand units a year were necessary to break even.

QUESTIONS

1. Would you accept this forecast of bar owners? Why or why not?
2. What are the advantages and disadvantages of using the opinions of dealers to forecast sales?

Part Three
THE MARKETPLACE AND BUYER PLANNING

The purpose of this part is to introduce the student to the processes involved in selecting market targets. Various types of demographic characteristics are used to show the types of market targets that should be considered separately. The important fact that the student should learn from considering market segments such as consumer goods or industrial goods markets, urban or rural markets, or young or old purchasers is that these submarkets are dynamic in size and characteristics. The successful marketer is the one who is aware of these variations and is able to estimate their impact on the success of his marketing mix. The marketer must constantly evaluate the market target he has selected to serve. He should select the market that he feels best fits the resources and objectives of his firm.

When deciding upon the market target for a firm, the logical starting place is a definition of the total market for the product (such as an automobile) or benefit (such as transportation) the company offers. This definition of the total market for the product, such as an automobile, will not encompass all people, as some do not have the *purchasing power* for an automobile or the *authority to spend the purchasing power*. The three prerequisites for a market to exist are (1) people, (2) purchasing power, and (3) authority to buy.

One broad distinction between potential customers in a total market is whether the product is purchased and used by an ultimate consumer or purchased to be used to produce a product for resale. This division of markets into *consumer* and *industrial* markets is not product-specific, as many products are sold in both markets. These two types of markets do vary on several dimensions.

Industrial purchases may involve more time, people, and specialized purchasing agents than do consumer purchases. As a result, the seller of industrial goods must plan his marketing mix accordingly. Industrial buyers also differ from consumer goods buyers in that they are fewer in number and more geographically concentrated. The more compact market makes access through a personal sales force economically feasible.

The existence of systematic purchasing procedures becomes the rule when the industrial goods market is considered. One segment of the industrial market, the government, is especially formalized in its purchasing processes. This segment, which accounts for approximately 80 percent of the $325 billion industrial market, generally requires that sellers become involved in competitive bidding.

Even the consumer goods market is not homogeneous. Many characteristics can be used to segment consumer goods buyers into groups that are best served by different marketing mixes. These characteristics include *geographical location*, *age*, *income*, and *stage in the family life cycle.*

People who are the same age, earn the same amount of income, and share other demographic characteristics may not exhibit homogeneous consumption behavior. Use of demographic characteristics for segmentation purposes often understates the impact of consumer motivations, perceptions, attitudes, and reference groups on consumption behavior.

The variations in seemingly similar, demographically segmented consumers become more evident if a broad, contemporary view of the consumption process is adopted. This contemporary view considers the act of purchasing a good or service as only one part of the consumption process. Consumption behavior should be broadened to include "all the acts of individuals in *obtaining* and *using* goods and services." The mental processes and physical actions that occur from the time a potential consumer recognizes a need until he has consumed a product and evaluated its performance are included in this broad view of consumer behavior.

The two general forces determining the character of consumer behavior are influences from within the consumer and those from the environment. These two forces are important both as separate forces and as combined forces. It is very difficult to discuss the two as distinct, noninteracting forces.

Several conceptual areas are discussed in relation to personal influences on consumer behavior. The first personal aspect examined is the concept of needs and motives. A need is the lack of something useful. A person without a bathroom in his house could be said to *need* an in-house facility. Several of the needs a person possesses may not affect his behavior at a given time because these needs may be considered relatively unimportant.

Conversely, if the consumer becomes convinced that the thing he lacks is important and needs to be satisfied, he will be *moved* to act. This need that has motivated him has now become a *motive*.

Two concepts relevant to motivation are self concept and type of needs. A person's motivations depend upon his mental conception of self. If he assesses his *self*-image or *looking-glass* image and feels it is too distant from the *ideal self*, he may be *moved* to act.

The relative impact of the concept of self upon behavior may be dependent upon the person's needs. Maslow's theory of hierarchy of needs intimates that people first emphasize the satisfaction of physiological needs and will only consider safety, belongingness, esteem, and self-actualization needs after these basic needs are at least partially satisfied. A person may not be concerned with trying to fulfill his ideal self until the need for self-actualization becomes activated.

Perception, a personal influence concept, is the *meaning attributed to incoming stimuli.* The attributed meaning is dependent upon the characteristics of both the stimuli and the person receiving the stimuli. The marketer's concern with perception focuses on understanding the processes by which consumers filter out some stimuli and how they interpret the stimuli that are received. It appears unlikely that stimuli such as advertisements introduced at the subconscious level are strong enough or introduced for a long enough period of time to gain the attention of the receiver. Moreover, subliminal advertising is generally not effective with groups of people, as wide variations are observed in individual perceptual thresholds.

Attitudes are a person's evaluations, feelings, or tendencies to act toward some object or idea. The marketer realizes that a consumer will probably not buy his product if he *evaluates* it as not as good as other brands, *feels* it is lousy, or has a *negative action* tendency toward the product. Consumer attitudes are measurable by the semantic differential technique. Once the attitudes are measured, the marketer should realign his marketing mix so that his market target is satisfied. Revision of marketing mix is generally preferable to attempting to change attitudes.

Social groups influence an individual's needs, motives, perception, and attitudes. The influence of the group on an individual depends upon the individual's status and role in the group. Group influence is greatest for products that are easily identifiable and socially conspicuous.

Social class is another type of group influence in addition to reference group influence. Social class is determined by occupation, source of income, education, family background, and dwelling area.

Family and culture are two other sources of influences on consumer behavior that emanate from outside the consumer. Family influence changes as the family's stage of the family life cycle changes. Culture is a societal force that extends beyond smaller subcultures and groups. The completely learned complex of values, ideas, attitudes, and other meaningful symbols that comprises culture encompasses attitudes toward such varied objects and ideas as religion, food, external personal appearance, and success.

PROGRAMMED REVIEW

1. We have defined marketing as the ________________________________

____

____

____

provision and efficient distribution of goods and services for chosen consumer segments

2. According to this definition, before designing a marketing mix a marketer must first
   ( ) produce a product.
   ( ) choose a price.
   ( ) hire a salesman.
   ( ) identify, evaluate, and select a market target.
   ( ) do a marketing research study.

identify, evaluate, and select a market target

3. Prior to selecting a market target, the marketer should know that there are three prerequisites for a market. A market exists if there are
   (a) people
   (b) ________________________________
   (c) ________________________________

(b) purchasing power

(c) authority to buy

4. A large proportion of the world's population, such as the relatively poor Asian masses, would not be considered part of the market for luxurious mink coats or yachts. These people do not qualify as a market because they do not have ________________________ or ________________

____

purchasing power

authority to buy

5. One way of segmenting markets is to divide them into consumer and industrial markets. The major reason for separating these two types of markets is that they may require ________________________ marketing mixes.

different

6. An example of a difference in marketing mix for industrial and consumer

buyers is the type of promotion used. Personal salesmen are ______________ more/less likely to be used by industrial sellers because industrial buyers are ______________ and ______________

____

more likely

concentrated

fewer in numbers

7. If consumer and industrial markets are separated, the seller must be able to classify buyers into one category or the other. The major criterion used to make this classification is the purchaser's ______________ for buying the good.

reason

8. If the ______________ the buyer purchases the product is to consume it himself, the product is a ______________ good. A person who buys an automobile for his own use is considered part of the ______________ market. Conversely, a company that buys cars for its salesmen to help in marketing its product is considered part of the ______________ market.

reason

consumer

consumer goods

industrial goods

9. A product is considered an industrial good if the buyer's reason for purchase is ______________

____

____

____

to use the good to produce other goods for resale

10. As mentioned in Question 6 above, industrial goods buyers are fewer in number and more geographically concentrated than consumer goods buyers. In addition, industrial goods buyers may require sellers to go through a set of steps such as entering bids when dealing with them. This formalized set of purchasing procedures established by industrial purchasers exemplifies the more ______________ nature of industrial purchases.

systematic

11. Many characteristics of a market can result in differences in the consumption behavior of market members. An important change in the United States market has been the movement of the population from ______________ to ______________ areas. The increased proportion of the population living in urban areas has undergone a shift within the ______________ areas.

rural

urban

urban

12. The shift occurring within urban areas involves movement from central cities to ______________ .

suburbs

13. As a result of the spreading of urban population farther and farther from the central city, defining markets in terms of traditional ______________

________ boundaries is meaningless. To accommodate urban and marketing planners, the Census Bureau has developed a classification system for urban areas called ________.

political

standard metropolitan statistical area

14. A standard metropolitan statistical area is
( ) an integrated economic unit.
( ) a city or twin cities of fifty thousand or more inhabitants.
( ) an integrated social unit.
( ) all of the above.

all of the above

15. A marketer who is interested in the characteristics of all people living around Philadelphia, Pennsylvania who are socially and economically integrated with activities of the central city should review statistics made available for the ________ of Philadelphia.

standard metropolitan statistical area

16. A marketer who separates the market into young children, teenagers, and adults is using the characteristic of ________ to segment his market.

age

17. Many differences have been observed in the consumption patterns of different-aged consumers. Some products are purchased or consumed almost entirely by one age segment. For example, the age segment that probably accounts for the majority of phonograph record sales is the ________ ________ segment.

school children or 6–19

18. Family life cycle is another method used for market segmentation. The variables used to determine if a consuming unit belongs to the bachelor, full nest, empty nest, or solitary survivor stage are

(a) ________ of household head,
(b) ________ status,
(c) ________ or ________ of children, and
(d) ________ of children.

(a) age

(b) marital

(c) presence or absence

(d) age

19. Various marketing implications have been drawn from the concept of family life ________. If a realtor wants to choose those people who are most likely to purchase a house, he should focus upon families in the stage of ________.

cycle

full nest I—youngest child under six (Figure 4–8)

20. Families with children all under six years of age are generally most likely to be in the market for a house. In addition, these families will be in the market for products for young children, such as ________ ________, ________, and ________ ________.

baby food vitamins toys (Figure 4—8)

21. All families with a full nest may not be in the market for a house. One very important reason for not being in the market is that some families may lack purchasing power or sufficient ________________.

income

22. Income is another characteristic that may be used to segment markets. The amount of income a person has will definitely affect his total level of expenditures. In addition, a person's expenditures for nonessential items depend upon the amount of ________________ income the person has.

discretionary

23. Discretionary income refers to the amount that the household has left after ________________ have been purchased.

necessities

24. One trend noticeable in the incomes of United States households has been ________________ discretionary spending power.

rising

25. Relative expenditures for food, household-related items, clothing, and other items tend to follow a pattern as family income changes. The first formal statement of these income-expenditure patterns was ________ ________ laws.

Engel's

26. Engel's observations of German peasants resulted in his proposed laws. The aspect of his law related to food expenditures, which has generally held true for other economies, is that the percentage spent for food will ________ ________ as income increases.

decrease

27. A recent survey of United States consumer expenditure patterns did not support Engel's contention that the percent of income spent for clothing will remain constant as income goes up. In the United States, families with increased incomes ________________ the percentage of their income spent for clothing.

increase (Table 4—4)

28. Another finding of the recent survey of expenditure patterns of the United States population that conflicts with Engel's laws concerns expenditures for medical and personal care. United States families generally ________ ________ the percentage of their income spent for medical and personal care as income increases.

decrease (Table 4—4)

29. One other relevant concept introduced in Chapter 4 is related to selection of market targets. The purpose of this concept, market grid, is to help the marketer ________________ and ________ ________ potential market targets.

isolate

evaluate

30. When constructing a marketing grid, several steps must be taken. First, the ________________ of ________________

must be chosen. These segmentation characteristics are used for the rows and columns of the grid. Next, the chosen segmentation variables such as age or income must be ________________.

basis of segmentation

divided

31. The purpose of the division of the characteristics into narrower ranges is to provide a basis for selecting ________________ market segments. Therefore, the degree to which the characteristic age is divided depends upon which age groups the marketer feels are ________________ in relation to his product.

homogeneous

homogeneous

32. Once the segmentation characteristics are chosen and divided, the potential of each segment must be determined. Once the potential of each segment is assessed, the marketer should
( ) select the largest segment.
( ) select the segment with the least sales potential.
( ) select the segment that will best enable the firm to accomplish its goals and objectives.

select the segment that will best enable the firm to accomplish its goals and objectives

33. A consumer's knowledge of his actions lies in three layers of consciousness. The white and gray areas are the conscious layers while the black area consists of nonverbal, ________________ emotions.

nonrational

34. If a person is questioned about his reasons for buying a sports car and these reasons lie in his black layer of consciousness, he will be ________________ to tell why he bought the car.

unable or unwilling

35. During the 1950s, a type of marketing research called motivation research was popularly acclaimed as the method to use to determine the motivations of buyers. This indirect method of measuring buyer motivations is based upon the assumption that motivations lie in the ________________ layer of consciousness.

black

36. As a result of difficulties encountered when directly questioning consumers about their motivations, it is necessary to view consumer behavior as a total process. Consumer behavior is viewed as a group of mental and physical processes carried out to obtain and use goods and services. A narrow view of consumer behavior is to examine only the actual ________________. This view overlooks events that ________________ and ________________ the purchase act.

purchase

precede and follow

37. The cause of this consumer behavior is the focus of Chapter 5. A symbolic statement of consumer behavior is $B = f(\_\_, \_\_)$.

P,E

38. The *P* represents personal influences that affect consumer behavior, while the *E* symbolizes the influencing forces outside the individual or the ________________ forces. An example of a force which

may affect the consumer's behavior is the ____________ ________ group within which the individual is born and raised.

environmental
family

39. A person will frequently alter his behavior so his friends will view him differently or so he can become more like what he wants to be. As a result, the individual's concept of ________________ influences his consumption ______________.

self
behavior

40. There are four components of the self-image. They are the ____________ ____________ self, self-____________, ____________ ____________ self, and ideal self.

real
image
looking-glass

41. The image of self a person aspires to become is his ____________ ____________ self. However, a person's current image of self may not be what he ideally wants or how he feels others view him. A person's conception of himself is his ____________ ____________, while his view of how others see him is his ______________.

ideal
self-image
looking-glass self

42. If a person feels that he needs to buy a new suit in order to fulfill his ideal self-image, this particular concept of self has led to a felt tension or an aroused need. This aroused need which serves as the driving force behind the consumer's behavior is a ______________.

motive

43. Motivations are aroused needs. A need may exist even though it does not ______________ a person to act. There may be other needs that are considered *more* important.

move

44. The needs that people experience are classified into five categories by Maslow. These five types of needs are arranged in a hierarchy within which they exert their influence. The first level of needs are ____________ ____________ needs such as the bodily needs for food and drink.

physiological

45. The other needs besides the physiological needs are ____________ ____________, ____________, ____________ ____________, and ____________.

safety
belongingness
esteem
self-actualization

46. A person may feel that he is currently satisfying his physiological needs but does not have enough security. His desire for security may also be called his safety need. One way to satisfy the safety need of protection against the risk of the death of the breadwinner is to purchase ____________ ____________.

insurance

47. A teenager may buy a motorcycle so that the members of a motorcycle gang let him belong. According to Maslow's hierarchy, the need that the teenager is trying to satisfy is the need for ______________.

belongingness

48. A person may have satisfied all of his needs except the need to develop his fullest potentialities and capacities. This highest-level need is the need for self-________________.

actualization

49. Many stimuli are sent by marketers to potential consumers. The meaning that people will attribute to these stimuli will depend upon their experiences, attitudes, beliefs, and other influencing forces. For example, Ralph Nader will probably not attribute the same meaning to the Chevrolet slogan, "Building a Better Way to See the USA" as will a loyal Chevrolet owner. This variation in the understanding of the stimuli reflects variation in ________________.

perceptions

50. There are two types of factors that explain our perception of an object. One of these factors explains the perceptual differences between Ralph Nader and the loyal Chevrolet owner. This difference arises from characteristics found in the person himself or ________________ factors.

individual

51. In addition to individual factors, perception may depend upon a characteristic of the ________________ such as the size of a magazine advertisement.

stimulus

52. All stimuli are not noticed by a given person. The likelihood of a ________________ being noticed is dependent upon the change in the stimulus as compared to the current level of ________________ ________________ of the stimulus. This relationship between noticeable differences and relative changes in the level of stimuli is known as ________________ law.

stimulus

intensity

Weber's

53. Weber's law is useful when explaining why all people may not notice a change in price, package contents, or size of advertisement. Some people may not notice a change in a stimulus because their perception of the original ________________ of the stimulus was higher than that of other people or the ________________ in stimulus intensity that will be noticeably different from the previous intensity is greater for these people.

intensity

smallest increase

54. Some stimuli are so contradictory to a consumer's present attitudes and opinions that the stimuli are not received at all. This unreceived information fails to penetrate the consumer's ________________ filter.

perceptual

55. As a review, the major concepts discussed to this point are levels of consciousness, concept of self, motives, Maslow's hierarchy of needs, perception, and Weber's law. To check your understanding, place the correct concept before each of the descriptions provided below.

________________ (a) Aroused needs that serve as the driving force behind consumer behavior.

_______________ (b) People try to satisfy physiological needs first, but these needs, if satisfied, are no longer motivators.

_______________ (c) A person's behavior depends upon how he feels others see him.

_______________ (d) Different people may attribute different meanings to the same stimuli.

_______________ (e) A person is more likely to notice a five-cent raise in the price of a candy bar than a five-cent raise in the price of an automobile.

_______________ (f) A person may not be able to explain his motivations because they may consist of nonverbal, nonrational emotions.

(a) motives
(b) Maslow's hierarchy of needs
(c) concept of self
(d) perception
(e) Weber's law
(f) levels of consciousness

56. Advertising designed to reach the receiver by aiming *below* the conscious level of awareness is _______________ advertising.

subliminal

57. Subliminal advertising may not be effective because
(a) strong _______________ factors are required to gain attention,
(b) only a _______________ message can be transmitted,
(c) individuals vary greatly in their _______________ of consciousness.

(a) stimulus
(b) very short
(c) thresholds

58. A person's perception depends upon his evaluations, feelings, or action tendencies toward the object that the stimuli concern. Another way to say this is that perception depends upon _______________.

attitudes

59. If a person likes the brand of a marketer, this person has a _______________ _______________ attitude toward this brand.

favorable

60. If a marketer discovers that consumers do not have a favorable attitude toward his brand, he should change the _______________ to match _______________.

product consumer attitudes	61. Attitudes are influences within the individual that influence behavior and groups are influencers of behavior that come from ______________ ______________ the individual. The influence of a group depends upon the individual's assigned status and role in that group. The rights and responsibilities assigned by the group to an individual are his ______________ ______________ in the group.
outside role	62. Groups can influence an individual's behavior even if the individual is not a group member. A group with which an individual identifies and one that he uses for standards of performance is a ______________ group.
reference	63. Group influence depends upon the characteristics of the product. Group influence is greatest if the item can be ______________ by others and is ______________.
identified conspicuous	64. An example of a product owned by everyone and therefore not socially conspicuous or influenced by group pressures is ( ) cars. ( ) clothing. ( ) drugs. ( ) canned peaches. ( ) air conditioners.
canned peaches	65. The social-class membership of a consumer influences his consumption behavior. ______________ distinct social classes have been identified in the United States by Warner. The class that accounts for the largest percent of the total population is the ______________ ______________ class.
six upper-lower	66. Many variations are observed among members of different classes. One class is very likely to buy new cars, large color television sets, and a kitchen full of appliances. This is the ______________ class.
lower or working	67. Social class is determined by ______________, source of income, ______________, family background, and dwelling area. One variable that is not considered in determining a person's social class is the amount of ______________.
occupation education income	68. It is difficult to determine what social class a family earning $15,000 a year is in because ______________ is not a ______________ ______________ of social class.
income determinant	69. The variables used to determine social class are (a) ______________ (b) ______________

(c) ____________________

(d) ____________________

(e) ____________________

(a) occupation
(b) source of income
(c) education
(d) family background
(e) dwelling area

70. Two major psychological differences between members of the lower and the middle social classes concern the rationality and self-confidence in decision-making ability. Generally, the middle class member is more ____________ ____________ and ____________ -confident in decision making.

rational
self
(Table 5–3)

71. The family is a group that influences consumer behavior and this influence changes over time. The role of food purchaser is generally assigned to the ____________.

wife

72. The role of actual purchaser of a refrigerator or car is generally assigned to the ____________ and ____________ ____________.

husband and wife

73. The member of the family who generally has the strongest influence on the style of car or refrigerator bought is the ____________ ____________.

wife

74. In America, we may say that the purpose of food is nourishment and the ideal appearance is one of slender youthfulness. These society-wide values represent part of the United States ____________.

culture

75. Culture is defined as the complex of ____________, ideas, ____________, and other meaningful symbols created by man to shape ____________ behavior and the artifacts of that behavior as they are ____________ ____________ from one generation to the next.

values
attitudes
human
transmitted

76. Within a culture several variations of cultural traditions, mores, and customs may exist. These smaller subcultures must be recognized by marketers because they may represent ____________.

distinct market segments

77. The consumer decision-making process should be considered as a conceptual model so that new research findings can be integrated with existent research to provide a more ____________ explanation of

________________ the individual behaves as he does. This conceptual model starts when an ________________ creates tension.

complete

why

unsatisfied basic determinant

78. As the decision-making process progresses, the consumer may decide to complete each stage and move to the next one or he may decide to ________________ the process.

halt

79. There are many reasons why a consumer may not make a purchase although an unsatisfied basic determinant exists. He may not purchase because he feels
(a) he has ________________ ,
(b) other ________________ are more important,
(c) presently available ________________ do not fit his needs,
(d) he cannot ________________ between alternatives.

(a) insufficient resources

(b) needs

(c) alternatives

(d) choose

80. If the purchase act occurs, other processes may take place after the purchase. The consumer will ________________ his purchase and the resultant ________________ .

evaluate

satisfaction

ASSIGNMENTS

1. Why is it important to distinguish between consumer goods and industrial goods?
2. Why is the concept of a standard metropolitan statistical area important to marketers?
3. Assume that you are planning to study the self-image of university students. What difficulties might you encounter when trying to measure each of the four components of self-image?
4. Provide an example of how each of the following influences perception:
   (a) attitudes
   (b) motives
   (c) reference group

5. Select a recent purchase you have made and describe the major aspects of the decision-making process you went through. Do your experiences fit the consumer decision-making model presented in the text?

CASELETS

1. The Fandastic Corporation

The Fandastic Corporation has developed a new type of detergent that does not contain any phosphates. The current problem facing the firm is to decide what market target it should choose in order to maximize its profits.

Management has provided the following information:

The two variables generally used by other firms selling a similar product are income and family life cycle. The levels of income used are low (zero to $4999 annual income), medium ($5000 to $10,000 annual income), and high (more than $10,000 annual income). The stages in the family life cycle used are bachelor stage, newly married, full nest, empty nest, and solitary survivor.

There are four firms that sell a product that will be directly competitive with Fandastic's new product. A sample of the members of each of the income-life cycle segments was selected and each person sampled was asked to try Fandastic's product and the four competitive products. These people were then asked to express their preference for the five products by ranking the most preferred as 1, and so on. The average rank assigned to Fandastic by each segment is shown in Table 1.

Table 1
RELATIVE PREFERENCE FOR FANDASTIC

	FAMILY LIFE CYCLE STAGE				
INCOME	BACHELOR	NEWLY MARRIED	FULL NEST	EMPTY NEST	SOLITARY SURVIVOR
Low	5	5	5	5	5
Medium	3	4	2	3	3
High	1	2	3	4	5

The estimated total *unit* sales of the four competitors for the last year are shown in Table 2.

Table 2
LAST YEAR'S SALES (IN THOUSANDS OF UNITS) FOR FOUR COMPETITIVE PRODUCTS

	FAMILY LIFE CYCLE STAGE				
INCOME	BACHELOR	NEWLY MARRIED	FULL NEST	EMPTY NEST	SOLITARY SURVIVOR
Low	5000	4000	10,000	5000	11,000
Medium	7000	6000	8000	7000	5000
High	3000	3000	5000	6000	3000

Finally, the company has estimated the costs of producing one million units of Fandastic and marketing it to each segment. The selling price has been set at $3.00 per unit.

Table 3
PRODUCTION AND DISTRIBUTION COSTS FOR EACH SEGMENT ($ MILLIONS)

	FAMILY LIFE CYCLE STAGE				
INCOME	BACHELOR	NEWLY MARRIED	FULL NEST	EMPTY NEST	SOLITARY SURVIVOR
Low	$1.2	$1.0	$2.0	$ .8	$1.0
Medium	.8	1.0	2.2	.7	1.2
High	.9	1.0	2.5	.6	1.5

QUESTIONS

1. Given this information, which market target should the firm choose? Why?
2. What additional information do you feel is necessary to make this market target decision? Why?
3. It may be difficult to actually obtain the data in the quantitative form presented in Tables 1, 2, and 3. Which of this information would be the most difficult to gather? the easiest?

2. The Condo Construction Company

The Condo Construction Company is trying to design a new condominium complex it is planning to build in a rural section of Pennsylvania. Although the area is essentially rural, it is located within ten miles of a city with a population of two hundred thousand and within forty miles of Baltimore and Philadelphia.

The company is trying to select its market target but it is unsure of what consumer characteristics to use for segmentation purposes.

The company has hired a newspaper-clipping firm to provide information about the advertisements of other condominium developers. Several headlines taken from recent condominium advertisements include, "Country-Style Living with Every Modern Convenience," "The Housing Opportunity of the Year FOR ONLY $1500 DOWN," and "Total Privacy and Carefree Living."

The decisions that the company desires to make include the precise location of the condominium complex; the inclusion or exclusion of recreational facilities, such as a golf course or swimming pool; disposition of the maintenance costs of the complex; the amount of square footage to put in the floor plan; and the exterior designs.

QUESTION

1. What characteristics do you think the Condo Company should use when determining the market target?

Part Four
PRODUCT STRATEGY

The firm's total planning begins with the product. Pricing structures, selection of marketing channels, and promotional plans are all based upon product planning. Even though these other variables in the strategy are important to the firm's success, none is more critical than the choice of products to offer potential customers.

A firm must take a marketing view of its product to be successful in today's competitive markets. The product must be viewed as a bundle of physical, service, and symbolic characteristics designed to produce want satisfaction.

A company planning to introduce a new product must concern itself with the various stages the product will pass through from the time of introduction to actual sales decline. The individual adoption process and the factors influencing the rate of adoption must also receive attention if the new product is to be accepted by consumers.

Products can be classified as either consumer or industrial goods. For efficient marketing, an understanding of the bases used to classify products and also how the classification of consumer goods can be extended to retail stores is essential.

Part Four also introduces the three basic product-market strategies available to the marketing manager as he attempts to match his product offerings with the needs of his chosen market target. Special emphasis is placed on the factors that influence the choice of a particular product-market strategy.

Attention is then focused on new products. The use and meaning of the word *new* is examined as are those factors that influence the decision to develop a line of products rather than concentrating on a single product.

The stages in the new product development process and four methods of organizing for new product development are reviewed to ensure a thorough knowledge of this subject.

The last topic treated in Part Four is the use of brand names, symbols, and packaging by companies to identify their products. Consumer knowledge and acceptance of brands are examined along with some commonly used branding terminology.

PROGRAMMED REVIEW

1. A product, from the marketing point of view, is defined as a bundle of physical, service, and symbolic characteristics designed to produce consumer *want satisfaction.* When a consumer buys a car, he is not buying the nuts, bolts, glass, nylon, and so on, that are embodied in the car; he is buying ______________.

want satisfaction

2. The three characteristics that produce want satisfaction are *physical, symbolic,* and *service.* The tangible product—the car—plus what the product enables the consumer to do—to move from place to place—are considered ______________ characteristics. The fact that the car has a prestigious brand name, well-thought-of by the consumer's friends, is a ______________ characteristic. The servicing of the car to fulfill the warranty requirements is a ______________ characteristic.

physical

symbolic

service

3. Products, like people, pass through a series of stages from the time they are introduced to the time they are no longer marketed. These stages are referred to as the product's life cycle. The typical life cycle of a product can be broken down into four distinct stages: *introduction, growth, maturity,* and *decline*. When a product first appears on the market, it is said to be in the ______________ stage. As sales volume begins rising rapidly and the firm begins making profits on the product, the product has entered the ______________ stage. When total-industry sales begin to reach a peak and competing products become more similar, the product is in the ______________ stage. In the final stage, total-industry sales decrease and new innovations begin replacing the product. This phase of a product's life cycle is referred to as the ______________ stage.

introduction
growth
maturity
decline

4. Although the lengths of the stages and the total length of the life cycle vary from one product to another, the product life cycle concept is extremely useful in marketing decision making. This concept provides insight into *future developments* as the product moves through the various stages. The product life cycle concept is useful in planning because it helps a manager anticipate ______________________________ in the marketing of a given product.

future developments

5. For example, as the product moves into the *growth* stage there is an increase in competitors, as other firms introduce competing versions of the product. An increase in the number of competing versions of the product usually occurs during the ______________________________ stage of the product life cycle.

growth

6. Anticipating this development would enable the marketing manager to *plan* for changes in the emphasis of his promotion from informative to competitive promotion. The insight provided by the product life cycle concept enables a manager to ______________________________ for changes in his marketing mix.

plan

7. When a new product is introduced, each individual consumer must decide whether or not he will buy the product. This decision-making process is referred to as the *consumer adoption process.* The decision-making process involved in adopting a new product is referred to as the _______________ _______________.

consumer adoption process

8. The consumer adoption process can be divided into the following stages: *awareness, interest, evaluation, trial,* and *adoption.* The consumer must first develop an *awareness* that the product exists. Then, in the *interest* stage, he seeks information about the product. After gathering information about the product, the consumer makes a mental *evaluation* of the product. A *trial* purchase is made if the evaluation is positive. Finally, the successful trial purchase leads to *adoption* of the product as a part of the consumer's purchase behavior.

Match the stages of the consumer adoption process given below with the statement that best describes each stage.

1. awareness	_____	(a) A mental consideration is made of the product.
2. interest	_____	(b) Consumer decides to make the product part of his buying behavior.
3. evaluation		
4. trial	_____	(c) Individual first learns of a new product.
5. adoption	_____	(d) A purchase (or demonstration) of the product is made to determine the usefulness of the product.
	_____	(e) Individual seeks information about the product.

3 (a)
5 (b)
1 (c)
4 (d)
2 (e)

9. The time period involved in carrying out this decision-making process varies from one consumer to another. However, when the total number of consumers who adopt a given product or service is considered, several distinct categories of consumers can be identified. These categories are based on the *relative time* of adoption. The categories of consumers who adopt a given product or service are based on the ____________ ____________ of adoption.

relative time

10. The first consumers to adopt a new product are called *innovators.* The innovators are followed by the *early adopters* who usually represent about 14–16 percent of the market. These two groups influence the *early majority*, the third category of adopters. The fourth group is called the *late majority* and together with the early majority represents about 68–70 percent of the market. The final category of adopters is called *laggards.* This is the last group to adopt the product. Using the graph below, identify the five categories of adopters as represented by each portion of the graph.

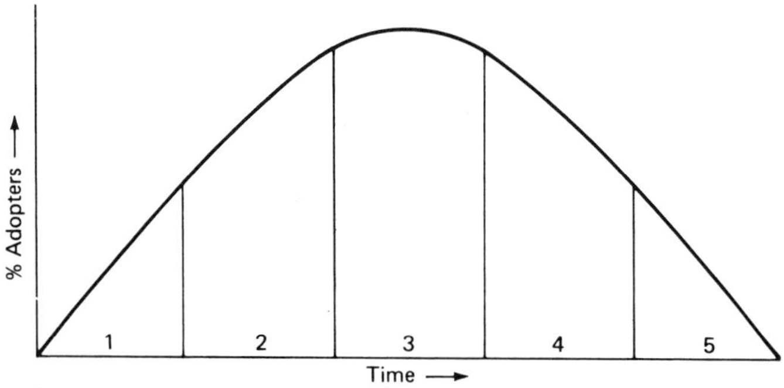

1. ____________
2. ____________
3. early majority
4 ____________
5. ____________

1. innovators
2. early adopters
3. early majority
4. late majority
5. laggards

11. Where possible, the identification of the consumers who are most likely to be *innovators* and *early adopters* can aid in the successful launching of a new product. Identifying and communicating with ____________ ____________ and ____________ can aid in making a new product successful.

innovators
early adopters

12. All products can be classified into two broad categories: consumer goods and industrial goods. Consumer goods are those products that are bought and used by ultimate consumers. Products destined for use by the ultimate consumer are called ____________.

consumer goods

13. Products that are used to produce other goods and services are called industrial goods. If a product is used to produce other goods and services, it is called an ______________________.

industrial good

14. The classification of consumer goods is based on the *buying habits* of consumers. Consumer goods are classified according to the ______________ ______________ of consumers.

buying habits

15. Thus, consumer goods are classified as *convenience goods, shopping goods,* or *specialty goods*, depending on how the majority of consumers buys a particular product. The three subcategories of consumer goods are
(a) ______________________ goods
(b) ______________________ goods
(c) ______________________ goods.

(a) convenience
(b) shopping
(c) specialty

16. *Convenience goods* are those goods that consumers want to purchase with a minimum amount of time and effort. The purchase of a soft drink at the nearest drink box would probably be considered a ______________ ______________.

convenience good

17. However, if the consumer purchasing a soft drink wanted only one particular brand of soft drink and was willing to go to several places to find this particular brand, the purchase would best be described as the purchase of a specialty good. Those products for which the consumer is willing to put forth great effort to acquire and for which he will refuse to take substitutes are referred to as ______________________.

specialty goods

18. *Shopping goods* are those products that the consumer purchases after giving careful consideration to the price and quality of several competing products. The purchase of an automobile, that was made after comparing the price and various features of several competing makes of cars, would be considered a ______________________.

shopping good

19. The classification of *industrial goods* is based on product use rather than buying behavior of consumers. Product use determines the classification of ______________________.

industrial goods

20. Industrial goods are classified into five categories: *installations, accessory equipment, fabricated parts* and *materials, raw materials,* and *supplies.* For each of the statements given below, write in the type of industrial good that best fits the description of product use.
(a) *Supplies* are regular expense items that are used in day-to-day operations of the firm, but do not become a part of the final product.
(b) ______________________ are a firm's capital assets such as factories, heavy machinery, and so on. These products do not become part of the final product.

(c) ______________________ is usually less expensive and shorter-lived than installations. This category includes such products as typewriters, hand tools, and so on.

(d) ______________________ and ______________________ do become a part of the final products and may undergo further processing before being incorporated into the end product. These include items such as radiators, hub caps, vinyl upholstering material, and fan belts.

(e) ______________________ are similar to fabricated parts and materials in that they do become part of the final products. Included in this category are farm products and natural products.

(a) supplies
(b) installations
(c) accessory equipment
(d) fabricated parts and materials
(e) raw materials

21. As was pointed out in Chapter 6, consumers buy products to have their needs satisfied. A company's basic objective is to offer products that *satisfy customer needs.* Consumers want their needs satisfied and companies want to offer products that ______________________.

satisfy customer needs

22. The process of attempting to match product offerings with customer needs is referred to as the *product-market matching process.* Matching product offerings to customer needs is referred to as the ______________________.

product-market matching process

23. There are three basic product-market strategies a firm can use to reach the objective of satisfying customer needs: *undifferentiated marketing, market segmentation,* and *concentrated marketing.* The three product-market strategies are

(a) ______________________ marketing
(b) market ______________________
(c) ______________________ marketing.

(a) undifferentiated
(b) segmentation
(c) concentrated

24. A company that markets one product to all consumers is following a strategy of *undifferentiated marketing.* Trying to meet the needs of all consumers with one product is referred to as ______________________.

undifferentiated marketing

25. If a company marketing vacuum cleaners had only one model that it tried to sell to all consumers, it would be following a strategy of ______________________.

undifferentiated marketing

26. A firm that develops separate products to satisfy smaller segments of the market is said to be following a strategy of *market segmentation.* Dividing

the market into smaller segments and developing separate products for each of the segments is called ______________________.

market segmentation

27. If the vacuum cleaner firm developed one model for the elite market, another model for the mass market, and still another model for the very price-conscious market, it would be following a strategy of ______________ ______________.

market segmentation

28. The other product-market strategy a firm may follow involves dividing the market into segments and then trying to satisfy the needs of only one of these segments. This is called *concentrated marketing.* Concentrating on a smaller segment of the total market is called ______________ ______.

concentrated marketing

29. If the vacuum cleaner firm referred to earlier segmented the market into the elite segment, the mass-market segment, and the very price-conscious segment and then concentrated on satisfying the needs of only those consumers in the price-conscious segment, it would be following a strategy of ______________________.

concentrated marketing

30. The particular product-market strategy chosen by a firm depends on several factors. These factors include *company resources, product homogeneity* as perceived by consumers, the *stage of the product's life cycle,* and the *strategies of competitors* already in the market. The four basic factors influencing the choice of the product-market strategy to be used by a firm are
(a) ______________________ resources
(b) stage of the ______________________
(c) product ______________________ as perceived by consumers
(d) ______________________ used by ______________
______________ already in the market.

(a) company
(b) product's life cycle
(c) homogeneity
(d) strategies competitors

31. Most firms do not produce and market a single product but develop a line of products. One of the factors influencing the decision to develop a complete line of products is the desire to grow. A firm limits its growth potential by concentrating on one product. Therefore, a company may develop a line of products because of a ______________________.

desire to grow

32. It may be possible for a firm to spread the costs of operating the company over several products and therefore reduce average costs. This would lead to optimum use of company resources. Another factor influencing the decision to develop a line of products is the attempt to attain ______________ ______________.

optimum use of company resources

33. A firm may be able to offer complementary or related products under its brand name and thus increase company importance in the market. Offering

a complete line of products rather than concentrating on a single product may ______________.

increase company importance in the market

34. The final factor influencing product-line planning is the exploitation of the product life cycle. Since every product eventually reaches the decline stage, a company with only one product faces eventual sales decline and extinction. Through ______________ a firm may avoid sales decline by continually introducing new products.

exploitation of the product life cycle

35. The introduction of "new" products by a company does not necessarily mean products that have not appeared on the market. A product can be new to consumers or new to a company. A new product may be defined as a product that is new to ______________ or new to a ______________.

consumers

company

36. The introduction of new products, whether new to consumers or to a company, can be extremely risky. An important prerequisite for efficient product innovations is a functioning organizational arrangement. Stimulating and coordinating new product development requires a functioning ______________.

organizational arrangement

37. The four most commonly used organizational arrangements for locating responsibility for new product development are *new product committees, new product departments, product managers*, and *venture teams.* List the four methods used to locate organizational responsibility for new product development.

(a) ______________

(b) ______________

(c) ______________

(d) ______________

(a) new product committees

(b) new product departments

(c) product managers

(d) venture teams

38. After developing the appropriate organizational arrangement for new product development, management should establish specific *procedures* for evaluating new product ideas. New product ideas should be evaluated through specific ______________ developed by management.

procedures

39. The new product development process may be thought of as consisting of six stages: *new product idea generation; screening; business analysis;*

product development; test marketing; and *commercialization.* Match the stages of the new product development process with the statement given below that best describes that particular stage.

1. new product idea generation
2. screening
3. business analysis
4. product development
5. test marketing
6. commercialization

_____ (a) This stage enables management to determine consumer reaction under simulated marketing conditions.

_____ (b) Product ideas are converted into a physical product.

_____ (c) This stage involves separating ideas with potential from those that do not meet company objectives.

_____ (d) The ideas for new products emerge at this stage.

_____ (e) Actual analysis of specific product ideas is conducted to determine potential, growth rate, and compatibility with company resources.

5 (a)
4 (b)
2 (c)
1 (d)
3 (e)

40. At each stage prior to commercialization, management must decide whether to *abandon the project, continue to the next stage,* or *seek more information* before proceeding further. What are the three alternatives available to management at each stage prior to commercialization?

(a) ______________________.
(b) ______________________.
(c) ______________________ before proceeding further.

(a) abandon the project
(b) continue to the next stage
(c) seek more information

41. All products must be identified by the companies marketing them. This is done through the use of brand names, symbols, and distinctive packaging. Marketers identify their products through the use of ______________ ______________, ______________, and ______________ ______________.

brand names
symbols
distinctive packaging

42. A brand is a name, term, symbol, design, or some combination of these used to identify the product of a particular company. A brand name is that part of the brand that can be vocalized. The words or letters comprising a name used to identify a product are referred to as a product's ______________ ______________.

brand name

43. It is important that a company's brand(s) be accepted by consumers. Brand acceptance may be measured in three stages: *brand recognition; brand preference;* and *brand insistence.* List the three stages of brand acceptance.

(a) ______________________

(b) ______________________________

(c) ______________________________

(a) brand recognition

(b) brand preference

(c) brand insistence

44. Brand recognition is the first objective of newly introduced products. When consumers are aware that a brand exists but are not predisposed to buy that brand, the brand has achieved the stage of ______________________.

brand recognition

45. Brand preference is the second stage of brand acceptance. Consumers will choose this brand if it is available. If this brand is not available, a substitute brand may be purchased. Choosing a particular brand, if available, is referred to as ______________________.

brand preference

46. When a consumer becomes so convinced of a product's merits that he will accept no alternatives, a brand has reached the stage of brand insistence. Consumers who buy only a particular brand are said to be at the stage of ______________________.

brand insistence

47. Brands may be classified as family brands or individual brands. A family brand is one used for several products. Campbell's Vegetable Soup and Campbell's Pork and Beans are examples of the use of ______________________.

family brands

48. An *individual brand* is one used for only one product. Although Procter and Gamble markets several different detergents—Tide, Cheer, Oxydol, and so on—each has its own brand name. This is an example of the use of ______________________.

individual brands

49. Some wholesalers and retailers offer their own brands of products that compete with the brands of manufacturers. These are called *private brands.* Manufacturers' brands are commonly called *national brands.* Sears' Die-Hard battery would be called a ______________________, while Chevrolet's Monte Carlo would be called a ______________________.

private brand

national brand

ASSIGNMENTS

1. The product life cycle consists of four stages: introductory stage, growth stage, maturity stage, and decline stage. For each stage of the life cycle given below, specify a consumer product that is in that particular stage. Briefly

explain what characteristics of the market for the product led you to place it in that stage.

(a) Introductory stage

(b) Growth stage

(c) Maturity stage—*Automobiles—slow growth in industry sales, little difference between competing models in the same price range, and promotional emphasis on minor differences.*

(d) Decline stage

2. The text points out that the classification of consumer goods can be extended to retail stores. Combine the product-store classifications, to give nine possible types of consumer purchase behavior as shown in the following matrix.

	STORES		
GOODS	CONVENIENCE	SHOPPING	SPECIALTY
Convenience			
Shopping			
Specialty			

Identify retail stores in your area that carry products that would indicate that consumers consider them (1) convenience store-convenience good or (2) shopping store-shopping good. Explain why the particular stores and products you identified would fit in that cell.

(a) Convenience store-convenience good

(b) Shopping store-shopping good

3. Identify at least two consumer products that have failed recently (been dropped by a company). Attempt to explain why these products failed by relating them to material in the text on product life cycles and the adoption process.

   (a) Product

   Reason for failure

   (b) Product

   Reason for failure

4. Locate promotional brochures on a relatively new consumer product. After reading through the brochures, try to determine how each of the following factors will influence the product's rate of adoption.

   (a) Relative advantage

   (b) Compatibility

   (c) Complexity

(d) Divisibility

(e) Communicability

5. For each of the situations given below, specify a product-market strategy that would be appropriate under the conditions described.

   (a) A small company is considering entering the market for watches. Although limited in financial resources that can be devoted to marketing watches to consumers, the company feels it has the production resources to develop a watch for use primarily by consumers interested in skin diving. The company currently markets a line of skin diving equipment including underwater depth gauges.
   What strategy would you recommend for this company? Why?

   (b) The Zeta Company was one of the first companies to introduce pneumatic drilling equipment in the industrial market. The product is now in the maturity stage and the company feels that it is necessary to adjust its undifferentiated marketing strategy.
   Although its earlier strategy has been successful, recent research evidence indicates that some industrial customers are not satisfied with the current products on the market. In fact, firms in the mining and construction industries have needs that are different enough to warrant completely different marketing mixes aimed at these customers.
   The Zeta Company is a well-established firm with adequate financial and production resources to develop a diversified line of products.
   What product-market strategy would you recommend for the Zeta Company? Why?

6. Obtain the package of a consumer product (perhaps one you recently purchased). Examine the package carefully and then try to determine

whether or not the package accomplished the tasks of promotion and protection given in Figure 7–8 of the text.

(a) Name of product and brief description of package.

(b) What promotional tasks were accomplished in your opinion?

(c) What protection tasks were accomplished in your opinion?

(d) How do you think the package could be improved? (from the standpoints of promotion and protection).

7. Given below is a list of factors that influence the demand for product-line expansion. Briefly explain how each factor influences the decision to expand a product line.

(a) A desire to grow

(b) Optimum use of company resources

(c) Increased company importance in the market

(d) Exploitation of the product life cycle

8. Make a trip to a local store—a grocery store or drug store would be best—and find a product available in both a manufacturer's brand and a private brand.

Examine the packages, descriptions of contents, and prices for both products. Then talk to the owner, manager, or other store personnel about the success of the two brands.

For this product, who is winning the "battle of the brands" in this particular store? Cite evidence that led you to your conclusion. (This may be sales information or customer feedback acquired from store personnel.)

(a) Product

(b) Manufacturer's brand(s)

(c) Private brand

(d) Evidence to indicate the winner on this particular "battleground"

CASELETS

1. Southland Industries

Ben West, a product manager for Southland Industries, was wondering what could be done with one of the firm's new products, Durafrest. Durafrest is a denture adhesive recently developed by the company as a byproduct of one of its major chemical products. Durafrest is an adhesive with tremendous holding power. In fact, the adhesive quality of the product was its major advantage over products currently used as denture fixatives.

The product had been on the market only a couple of weeks when complaints began to pour in from dissatisfied users. Evidently, the product worked too well! Users had great difficulty in loosening the adhesive once it was applied.

"Well, it looks like we're going to have to 'pull' Durafrest from the market," said Ken Kane, vice-president of production. "Surely there are some other uses of such an adhesive."

QUESTIONS

1. What was this company's definition of a product? How does this conflict with the views expressed in our text?

2. The King Kang Company

The King Kang Company markets a line of high-quality children's toys throughout the United States and Canada. These toys are usually sold in specialized toy stores and in a few department stores.

Since prices in these toy shops are higher than prices in the usual toy outlets, most of the clientele of these stores are placing greater emphasis on quality and service than on price when shopping. They prefer to shop at these particular outlets for their children's toys.

Research evidence gathered by the King Kang Company indicated that most children and parents who have purchased its line of toys continue to buy the King Kang brand in future toy shopping.

QUESTIONS

1. What kind of consumer goods are represented by the King Kang Company's toy line?
2. What would be the product-store classification of King Kang toys purchased through one of the toy shops? Why?

3. The Ling Company

The Ling Company, founded in 1908, was one of the oldest manufacturers of shampoo in the nation. Its well-known brand, Linger, had been a leading seller. However, as more and more firms entered the shampoo market, sales of Linger leveled off.

Linger had been conceived as an all-around shampoo for both men and women, to be used with all types of hair and scalp conditions. The newer entrants into the market seemed to be designing products for specific parts of the market. One firm had developed a whole line of women's shampoo for three different hair and scalp conditions—dry, oily, and regular. This company was doing quite well and, in fact, was expected to bring out a similar line of shampoos for men within the next year.

Carl Jones, manager of the Ling Company, felt he must take some action immediately to change the current sales pattern.

QUESTIONS

1. What product-market strategy was used by the Ling Company?
2. Why did a seemingly successful strategy become inadequate?

4. The Tokay Manufacturing Company

In recent years, the Tokay Manufacturing Company has experienced several financial crises as a result of its failure to introduce new products. Competitors always seem to introduce the innovations and Tokay ends up copying these new products. By the time its new versions of the product are ready to be marketed, competitors are well-established in the innovations and Tokay competes mainly on the basis of price.

In the past, the president of Tokay had depended on salesmen and production personnel to come up with new product ideas. They would then be temporarily relieved of some duties to see their ideas through actual development and marketing.

This had caused difficulties not only in terms of shifting workloads around but also because it ended up that no one really had the responsibility for developing new products. The president knows something has to be done soon and so he has decided to try to determine how he might assign the responsibility for new product development within his organization.

QUESTIONS

1. How can the president of Tokay make sure someone is responsible for developing new products?

Part Five
DISTRIBUTION STRATEGIES

Marketing channels, the paths goods—and title to these goods—follow from producer to consumer, must be constructed and maintained by marketing managers. Channels are vital to the overall success of the firm's marketing program and much effort goes into their development and maintenance.

Knowledge of the nature and function of marketing channels is fundamental and must precede the development of channel strategy. Successful managers recognize the need to provide consumers adequately with the *utilities of time, place, and ownership* through effective channel management.

A prime task for any marketing manager is the construction or further development of his firm's marketing channels. Before beginning, however, he must obtain certain information and make several critical policy decisions. Knowledge of the functions and services provided by various middlemen, together with the channels used for certain types of consumer and industrial goods, is necessary. In addition, the manager must know why specific channels are used. Thus, consideration of all the *consumer, product, firm,* and *environmental factors* affecting channel choice is important, for they *constitute the fundamentals of channel strategy.*

Once the marketing decision maker has determined the channels he will use for a particular product, he must decide whether to follow a policy of *intensive, selective,* or *exclusive market coverage.* In making his choice, he is determining the number and geographic location of his retail outlets. It is important that he understand the reasons for the selection of a particular pattern of market coverage. *Consumer, product, firm,* and *environmental factors* are important variables in the determination of market coverage.

The choice of marketing channels and the selection of market coverage are only the beginning of the manager's job, for he must then construct and maintain his channels. The construction of channels includes the contact with middlemen, the development of a working arrangement, and the give-and-take of day-to-day operations. Working arrangements, for example, may involve legal problems for both seller and buyer. *Exclusive dealing contracts, closed sales territories,* and *tying contracts* are examples of potentially difficult legal arrangements.

Once a marketing channel has been constructed, the maintenance of cooperative relations among channel members is vital to the success of the channel. Although *cooperation* is necessary to reach the end goals of channel operations, *conflict* may arise for a variety of reasons. The development of strong leadership, such as a *channel captain,* in channels consisting of independent middlemen is, however, a positive influence leading to greater cooperation.

In addition to channels comprised of completely independent middlemen, there are three other types of channels, referred to collectively as *vertical marketing systems.* Unlike independent channel systems, these three types of vertical marketing systems—*corporate, administered,* and *contractual*—are centrally programmed and managed. All types of vertical marketing systems, especially contractual systems such as *wholesaler-sponsored voluntary chains, retail cooperative chains,* and *franchise organizations,* should be fully understood because they are growing in importance.

For a marketing channel to function, storage, selling, transportation, information, and financing services must be provided. *These functions may be performed by any member of the channel;* they can be shifted, but they cannot be eliminated.

The last part concentrated on the overall management of marketing channels. In this part, wholesaling and retailing are described and recent changes are noted along with an explanation for the changes.

Wholesaling, the institution most directly involved in breaking bulk and routing small orders to retailers, is the first marketing institution described. *This function may be performed by manufacturer-owned facilities* such as *sales offices* or *sales branches;* most often, however, it is performed by *independent wholesalers.* Manufacturers can also use *public warehouses, trade fairs, and exhibitions or merchandise marts.*

Unless it is economically feasible to perform the wholesaling function themselves, firms will use the services of an independent wholesaler. *Merchant wholesalers* are most often used. They take title to goods and perform a variety of services. Some perform many functions and are called *full-function merchant wholesalers.* In the industrial goods market, such wholesalers are called *industrial distributors.* The services of all wholesalers are tailored to meet the needs of their customers; for example, the *rack jobber* is a full-function merchant wholesaler who provides a unique service for grocery stores.

In many cases, retailers do not need the range of services that a full-function wholesaler can provide and in those cases wholesalers offering a limited number of specific services are used. These wholesalers are called *limited-function merchant wholesalers.* They include *truck jobbers*, *drop shippers*, and *cash-and-carry wholesalers.*

Truck jobbers routinely provide perishable items such as bread, tobacco, and candy to retailers who wish to maintain a small but fresh inventory for their customers. *Drop shippers* sell large, bulky, nonagricultural commodities and have them sent directly to the buyer. Although they take title, drop shippers do not physically handle the goods they sell. *Cash-and-carry wholesalers* sell grocery items to small retailers. As the name indicates, these wholesalers neither perform the delivery function nor extend credit.

Another type of independent wholesaler is the *agent wholesaler.* Agents usually perform few services and unlike merchant wholesalers they do not take title to goods. Agents aid the flow of goods through the marketing channel by bringing buyer and seller together. *Commission merchants, brokers, selling agents, and manufacturers' agents* are classified as agent wholesalers.

Commission merchants take possession of the agricultural products they sell and attempt to get the "best price" for the seller. *Brokers* can be used to find buyers or sellers. The one function of the broker is to bring buyer and seller together.

Selling agents provide many services for the firms they represent. Generally, they sell the entire output of the selling organization and quite often they comprise the firm's entire marketing effort. Thus, they have been called the independent marketing department, since they usually have great freedom in price setting and promotion. *Manufacturers' agents* are area specialists. These agents represent several companies carrying noncompeting lines. Manufacturers tend to use them when they wish to open a new territory or cannot afford to maintain a salesman in the territory covered by the manufacturers' agent.

Retailing, the final link in the marketing channel, is the second marketing institution described. Like wholesaling, retailing functions may be performed by any member of the channel. Manufacturers may sell direct through their own stores, by direct mail, or house-to-house selling. Wholesalers can also sell direct to the ultimate buyer as long as such sales do not make up a major part of their sales volume.

Since 97 percent of retail sales are made by retail stores, they warrant attention. *Limited-line stores and specialty shops* select and cater to specific market targets. *Department stores*, on the other hand, attempt to provide customers with one-stop shopping for all personal and household items. *Discount stores* attempt to do the same thing yet they have a different approach to customer service than department stores. Discount stores stress low prices and minimum service.

Retail market power is often found in *chain stores*, which are two or more stores centrally owned and managed. Chain stores dominate in certain areas of retailing such as variety stores, shoe stores, and department stores.

Change in retail institutions is an important subject for the marketer. *Scrambled merchandising* is a term used to denote one form of change. Retailers attempting to match changing consumer shopping patterns have expanded their assortments to include products not normally considered part of their offering. The gas station that sells groceries is an example of scrambled merchandising.

Another change of importance to marketers is the movement of retail stores to suburban locations, usually into planned *suburban shopping centers.* The growth of planned shopping centers that provide convenient parking and effective family shopping cannot be ignored by marketing managers.

The "*wheel of retailing*" hypothesis is one attempt to explain the evolution that occurs in retailing. According to this hypothesis, low-priced, minimum-service retailers mature by adding services and raising prices. The maturing retailing institutions provide the opportunity for new low-priced retailers to enter the retailing field. Although the "wheel of retailing" does not explain all the changes that have occurred in retailing, it does predict an evolution that has occurred in many cases.

Physical distribution is closely related to the marketing channel, for the proper physical flow of goods is a vital fact of an effective marketing channel. The functions of storage (warehousing), transportation, materials handling, inventory control, order processing, and customer service are important for the creation of the utilities of place, time, and possession.

It was not until the 1950s that the significance of efficient physical distribution was recognized and extensive effort made to integrate this area. The systems concept—total-cost approach, avoidance of suboptimization, and cost trade-offs —is used to improve the performance of physical distribution.

Physical distribution management works to deliver goods to the point of purchase at minimum cost while meeting a specified level of customer service. The physical distribution manager's job is not an easy one, for each of the functions or elements is complex. He must select the best combination of transportation mode, warehousing, materials handling, inventory level, order processing, and customer service. He may choose from among five transportation alternatives: railroads, motor carriers, water carriers, pipelines, and air carriers. He may use a combination of these alternatives and develop an intermodal transportation system such as birdyback, fishyback, or piggyback.

He has to determine the right number of warehouses and their location. Since warehouses are relatively permanent, this decision is important to the total cost of a particular physical distribution flow. Inventory costs are high and as a consequence, the physical distribution manager must keep inventory as low as possible while maintaining required service levels. An efficient *order-processing system* is relevant to efficiency of cost and service. An improper order system can cause the entire flow to be a burden rather than an effective aid to sales and marketing.

Like order processing, efficient *materials handling* is an integral part of physical distribution. Materials handling innovations such as *unitizing* and *containerization* have recently gained wide acceptance by shippers, carriers, and customers.

Automated warehouses, with a modern materials-handling system, using an accurate inventory-control model, an efficient, computerized order-processing system, and the proper transportation mode, combine to give specified consumer service and cost efficiency. Any marketing manager with these benefits will have a major component of his total marketing effort under control. This is true whether the market is foreign or domestic.

A properly operating physical distribution system can be a marketing plus, while an inefficient system can be a disaster. Every marketing manager should make the effort to understand his organization's physical distribution system and be constantly alert for opportunities to improve it.

PROGRAMMED REVIEW

1. Paths that goods—and title to these goods—follow from producer to consumer are known as marketing ________________.

channels

2. ________________ channels are very important to the firm for they bridge the gap between producer and ________ ________.

marketing
consumer

3. In moving goods to a location convenient for the consumer, ________ ________ provide time, ________________ and ownership utility.

channels
place

4. Time utility is extremely important when the firm is engaged in speculative production rather than job-order production. ________ ________ production is the rule, not the exception, today.

speculative

5. In addition to providing time utility by having products available *when* the customer wants to buy, the firm should provide the product *where* the customer wants to buy. By doing so, the firm provides ________ ________ utility.

place

6. The marketing channel that provides the customer with physical possession of the product and the ________________ to the goods performs the service of providing ownership ________ ________.

title
utility

7. A middleman is a firm operating between the ________ ________ and consumer or industrial purchaser and includes both ________________ and retailers.

producer
wholesalers

8. Wholesalers and retailers are defined by the purpose for which purchases are made. If a great majority of purchases is made by persons for their own use, the seller is considered to be a ________________.

retailer

9. There is no such thing as a "best marketing channel" for a particular product. ________________ should be developed after an analysis of consumer needs.

channels

10. Rather than being satisfied that the "best" channel has been found, it is advisable to remember that marketing channels are not static; they ________________ over time.

change

11. The simplest, most direct marketing channel is direct from ________ ________ to consumer or industrial user.

manufacturer

12. The traditional marketing channel, one that is used by literally thousands of small manufacturers, is from manufacturer to ________ ________ to retailer to consumer or industrial user.

wholesaler

13. Small retailers who use the traditional marketing channel generally rely on wholesalers as buying ________________ for them.

agents 14. In the marketing channels for small accessory equipment and operating supplies, ________________ are generally called industrial distributors.

wholesalers 15. An ________________ is a wholesaler who does not take title to goods; he merely represents the ________________ to the buyer.

agent

seller 16. The marketing channel consisting of manufacturer to agent to wholesaler to ________________ to consumer is often used when products are produced by a large number of companies.

retailer 17. In instances where unit sale is large and transportation costs are a small percentage of total product costs, the manufacturer to ________________ to industrial user channel may be employed.

agent 18. ________________ channels are becoming increasingly common in marketing today because one channel may not serve all the ________________ for a particular product.

multiple

markets 19. The choice of marketing channels from those available to a marketing manager should be made after an analysis of the ________________, the product, the firm, and the environment has been made.

consumer 20. Whether the product is an industrial good or a consumer good, the location and needs of the potential market and the shifts in consumer buying patterns are all ________________ factors.

consumer 21. Product perishability, unit value, and service requirements are characteristics of the ________________ that should be analyzed when determining channel structure.

product 22. The manufacturer's need for ________________ over his product and the breadth of the ________________ line are characteristics of the manufacturer (firm) that help determine channel length.

control

product 23. The nature and extent of competition and legal considerations are two ________________ factors that marketing managers should consider when selecting marketing channels.

environmental 24. The three degrees of market coverage are intensive, ________________, and exclusive.

selective 25. An extreme form of selective distribution is called ________________ distribution, because the manufacturer grants exclusive

______ rights to a wholesaler or retailer to sell in a geographic region.

exclusive

26. Exclusive-______ contracts prohibit a middleman from handling competitor's products. However, such contracts may be unlawful in those cases where they violate Section 3 of the ______ Act.

dealing

Clayton

27. When a manufacturer restricts the geographic territories for each of his distributors, he is said to have closed ______ territories and such action may be unlawful.

sales

28. Vertical territorial restrictions between a manufacturer and a ______ or retailer are generally legal, but ______ restrictions involving agreements among ______ or wholesalers to avoid competition have consistently been declared unlawful.

wholesaler

horizontal

retailers

29. Tying contracts that require an exclusive dealer for a manufacturer's products to carry other of the ______ products in inventory become violations of the Sherman and ______ Acts when they ______ competitors from major markets.

manufacturer's

Clayton

restrict

30. Retailers are assuming more and more the role of channel ______, as they have grown in size and power.

captain

31. The channel captain works to assure the level of ______ necessary for the channel to function properly. Nevertheless, ______ can often arise.

cooperation

conflict

32. Sometimes a manufacturer may use a ______ salesman to assist other channel members.

missionary

33. The three types of vertical ______ systems currently operating are corporate, ______, and administered.

marketing

contractual

34. In a corporate vertical marketing system, a single ______ owns each stage of the marketing channel.

firm

35. In an administered system, coordination is attained by a dominant channel member who is called a ______.

channel captain

36. The most significant form of vertical marketing system is the ______ system, which accounts for nearly 40 percent of all retail sales.

contractual

37. Three types of contractual ________ marketing systems exist; they are wholesaler-________ voluntary chains, retailer cooperatives, and franchise organizations.

vertical
sponsored

38. The franchise form that has created the most excitement is the ________-firm sponsored retailer franchise system.

service

39. Under the service-firm sponsored retailer franchise system, the franchiser provides a proven system of retailer operation and ________ prices for suppliers. In return, the franchisee pays a ________ for the name and a percentage of gross ________.

lower
fee
sales

40. Marketing ________ are made up of marketing institutions—wholesalers and retailers.

channels

41. These marketing ________ perform certain functions necessary for marketing channels to operate. ________ and ________ are the two institutions discussed in Chapter 9 of the text.

institutions
wholesalers
retailers

42. Wholesalers and retailers perform storage, bulk-breaking, contact, information, and financing ________ in the marketing ________.

functions
channel

43. By breaking bulk, that is by ________ large orders from suppliers into smaller shipments for retailers, wholesalers provide savings in transportation costs. If the manufacturer had to ship direct to each retailer, the cost of transportation would be much ________.

breaking
greater

44. By representing many manufacturers to a single customer, wholesalers and ________ reduce the number of transactions between the ________ and final buyer. And, since contacts cost money to make and maintain, total marketing costs can be lowered by using ________ and retailers.

retailers
manufacturer
wholesalers

45. In addition, because of their central position between manufacturer and consumer, ________ and ________ serve as information links.

wholesalers
retailers

46. Both wholesalers and retailers provide a financing function by selling on credit. By purchasing on ________, retailers may

obtain leverage; that is, they can realize a greater return on invested capital.

credit

47. Marketing functions performed by middlemen must be performed; the functions may be shifted from wholesaler to manufacturer, but they cannot be eliminated. For example, large manufacturers and retailers may perform their own wholesaling ____________.

functions

48. Wholesalers comprise an important part of our economy. There are three hundred eleven thousand ____________ establishments with total sales of nearly 500 billion ____________ in the United States.

wholesale

dollars

49. Wholesalers are classified by ownership into two categories: independent ____________ and manufacturer-owned.

wholesalers

50. The volume of products marketed by manufacturer-owned wholesaling facilities is increasing. Over 50 percent of all industrial goods and slightly more than one-third of all products are marketed through ____________ wholesaling facilities.

manufacturer-owned

51. Manufacturer ____________ operations are carried out through either a sales branch or a ____________ office. The major difference between these two wholesale facilities is the fact that the ____________ branch carries inventory while the sales office serves principally as an ____________ for salesmen.

wholesaling

sales

sales

office

52. Smaller manufacturers and large firms developing new territories may use public warehouses. For a fee, a ____________ warehouseman will perform wholesaling ____________ such as breaking bulk, packaging inventory to fill orders, and billing purchasers.

public

functions

53. In addition, manufacturers may market through trade fairs, exhibitions, and merchandise marts. Trade ____________ and exhibitions are held from time to time, while the merchandise ____________ is a permanent exhibition.

fairs

mart

54. The largest wholesaler group in both number and sales is independent wholesalers. The two categories of ____________ wholesalers are merchant wholesalers and agent ____________.

independent

wholesalers

55. Merchant ____________ take title to the ____________ they sell. They may be further classified as full or limited-function wholesalers.

wholesalers
goods

56. Full-________ merchant wholesalers provide a complete range of services for the buyer and are generally found in industries where retailers are small and carry a large ________ ________ of inexpensive items.

function
number

57. In the industrial goods market, the ________ ________-function merchant wholesaler is often called an ________ ________ distributor.

full
industrial

58. Supermarkets often use a rack jobber who provides special assistance in marketing high-margin, nonfood items about which the ________ ________ manager knows little. Rack ________ ________ also service drug, hardware, variety, and discount stores. This full-________ wholesaler provides the racks and merchandise, then prices and maintains the displays.

supermarket
jobbers
function

59. The limited-function ________ wholesaler provides specialized services that are designed to meet the needs of a segment of retail and industrial buyers.

merchant

60. One example of the limited-function wholesaler is the cash-and-carry wholesaler who provides merchandise at a low price but does not ________ it. Although successful in England, the service of the ________ wholesale operation does not appeal to the American chain-store manager.

deliver
cash-and-carry

61. Truck jobbers make regular deliveries of such items as bread, tobacco, and candy to retail ________. They perform basically the same functions that route salesmen would provide for a bakery; that is, ________ jobbers perform sales, delivery, and collection functions.

stores
truck

62. A drop shipper is not a clumsy freight handler; he is a limited-function merchant ________ who receives orders from customers and forwards them to producers who ship directly to the buyers. The ________ shipper never handles the goods he sells. He usually sells goods that are bulky and purchases are made in carload lots.

wholesaler
drop

63. Agent ________ do not take title to the goods they sell. They are, however, instrumental in bringing buyer and seller together and are important in completing the transaction.

wholesalers

64. The four major types of ________ wholesalers are commission merchants, brokers, selling ________ ________, and manufacturers' agents.

agent
agents

65. Commission ________________ sell agricultural products for producers. They not only take possession of the ________________ ________________ but attempt to obtain the "best price" possible for the owner.

merchants
product

66. Brokers provide one service. They bring buyer and ________________ ________________ together. Unlike the ________________ merchant, they can represent either the seller or the ________________ ________________. Generally, ________________ are not effective representatives for sellers seeking regular, continuing service.

seller
commission
buyer
brokers

67. Selling ________________ are ideal for the small, poorly financed, production-oriented ________________. The ________________ agent is capable of representing the seller on a continuing basis, selling all of the firm's output and even making price and promotion decisions.

agents
firm
selling

68. The manufacturers' ________________ is an independent salesman who has his own territory. A manufacturer may use ________________ ________________ agents to develop new territories or represent the firm in areas where it is inefficient for company salesmen to operate. The manufacturers' agent usually sells a line of related but noncompetitive products and represents several manufacturers in his territory.

agent
manufacturers'

69. Retailing, the sale of the product or service to the ultimate consumer for his own use, involves selling via retail ________________, telephone, mail order, automatic vending, and directly house-to-________________. Approximately 97 percent of retail sales are made in retail stores.

stores
house

70. ________________ stores attempt to match the needs of the buyer. For example, the first important retail institution was the general ________________. This was a general merchandise store that carried goods that met the needs of the small rural community. It provided a social as well as commercial service to its customers.

retail
store

71. While many stores are limited-line stores or specialty shops that cater to the needs of a specific market target, the symbol of retailing is the department ________________ which is a one-stop shopping store for all personal and household items.

store

72. ________________ stores began in the 1800s and are a well-established retailing institution. Since World War II, however, discount ________________ have evolved. The ________________ ________________ store stresses low price and minimum service. Recently, discount operations have been adding services and becoming similar to traditional ________________ stores.

department
stores
discount
department

73. Chain stores consist of two or more ________ that are centrally owned and managed. ________ ________ stores account for one-third of the dollar volume of retail sales and they are dominant in three fields: variety stores, department ________, and shoe stores.

stores
chain
stores

74. Recent trends in retailing include the growth of suburban shopping centers. Convenient and free parking and store locations planned to facilitate family shopping have given the suburban shopping ________ ________ a definite advantage over the older, downtown ________ areas. It is predicted that planned shopping centers will continue to grow.

center
shopping

75. Another fundamental change in retailing has been scrambled merchandising, the deterioration of clear-cut delineations of retailer types. ________ merchandising represents the retailer's attempt to satisfy the consumer demands for convenient, one-stop shopping.

scrambled

76. A major attempt to predict change in retailing is called the "wheel of retailing," which hypothesizes that new types of ________ ________ gain recognition by offering lower prices that are made possible by reducing or eliminating services. Over time, however, they add services and prices rise, which in turn makes them vulnerable to new, low-priced ________. However, the ________ ________ hypothesis does not explain all emerging patterns in retailing. For example, suburban shopping centers and vending machines did not grow on the basis of low-cost appeals.

retailers
retailers
"wheel of
retailing"

77. The broad range of activities included in the area of physical ________ ________ are those concerned with the movement of goods from the time they have been produced until they reach the consumer.

distribution

78. Today, physical distribution is important because it is one place where efficiency can be attained. During World War II, logistics techniques were developed that would later be applied to problems in ________ ________ distribution.

physical

79. During the 1950s, increasing transportation costs, expanding product lines, and changing stocking practices combined to force firms to recognize the need for ________ physical distribution.

efficient

80. The systems approach can be applied readily to problems of physical distribution. This ________ means that the firm must recognize the mutual interdependence of the basic functional areas of physical ________.

approach
distribution

81. Using the systems approach, the physical distribution manager makes use of three basic concepts—the total-cost approach, the avoidance of suboptimization, and the cost trade-offs concept—to reach his objective. In essence, his objective is to minimize ______________________ while maintaining a specified level of customer service.

cost

82. The first concept, the total- ______________________ approach, stresses that the manager should consider the costs of all functions as a whole.

cost

83. In avoiding sub ______________________, the manager must attempt to optimize the total physical ______________________ effort, rather than any one part.

optimization
distribution

84. Often by increasing the cost of one function, the cost of another function will decrease even more, with the net result a ______________________ in total cost. This is an example of the use of cost ______________________.

decrease
trade-offs

85. These three basic concepts—the ______________________ approach, the ______________________ of suboptimization, and the use of ______________________ trade-offs—constitute the foundation of the physical distribution concept.

total-cost
avoidance
cost

86. Integrating the physical ______________________ area is a difficult task that is more easily accomplished by bringing all the functions under the direction of one person and therefore centralizing decision making.

distribution

87. Two factors that support the move to ______________________ decision making are the savings obtained by freight consolidation and the need to be near the firm's central computer facilities.

centralize

88. A physical distribution system includes transportation, warehousing, inventory control, customer service, order processing, and materials handling sub ______________________.

systems

89. One of the most difficult problems facing a manager when choosing a transportation mode is determining the cost of the service. Since the ______________________ industry is regulated by the government, shipping charges are also ______________________. Tariff books that contain the charges are so complicated that firms known as freight bill auditing companies exist to detect errors.

transportation
regulated

90. There are two basic types of freight rates: class and commodity. Class ______________________ are standard rates for every commodity moving between two places. ______________________ rates are allowed to be given by carriers to shippers for large-quantity shipments or regular use.

rates
commodity

91. There are three basic classifications of carriers: common, contract, and private. Common ________________ serve the general public while contract carriers do not. ________________ carriers work only for certain customers. Private carriers transport products only for their own use.

carriers
contract

92. There are five transportation alternatives open to the physical ________________ manager: railroads, trucks, water carriers, pipelines, and airlines.

distribution

93. Railroads are the largest transporters, as they move the largest amount of freight and are one of the most efficient methods for moving bulk commodities. ________________ offer special services such as run-through trains and unit trains.

railroads

94. The trucking industry has grown rapidly over the past decades. ________________ offer fast, consistent service.

trucks

95. Pipelines are second only to railroads in number of ton-miles transported. Advancement is being made in an effort to move a greater diversity of products by ________________ .

pipeline

96. Airlines are used to transport items that are valuable or highly perishable. ________________, however, account for only one-fifth of 1 percent of the total ton-miles shipped.

airlines

97. Transportation modes are also combined to provide better service. Piggyback, fishyback, and birdyback are the names used to describe these innovations. Piggyback, the most common, involves the combination of the trucking and railroading industries. Truckers and water carriers combine to provide ________________ service. When motor and air carriers combine efforts it is called ________________ .

fishyback
birdyback

98. The number and location of warehouses are important considerations in physical ________________. Not only are products stored in warehouses, they are also redistributed from them. ________________ are classified as either storage warehouses or distribution warehouses.

distribution
warehouses

99. As the name indicates, storage warehouses are used to ________________ goods. Distribution warehouses, on the other hand, serve as a place to assemble and redistribute goods.

store

100. With the aid of the computer, warehouses are often automated. That is, an ________________ materials-handling system is employed in the warehouse.

automated

101. The location of warehouses is a major decision for a firm. It is a complex

decision involving the analysis of two general costs: warehousing and materials- ____________________ costs and delivery ____________________.

handling
costs

102. Additional factors in the ____________________ decision include taxes, laws and regulations, labor-force availability, police and fire protection, available transportation, and community acceptance.

location

103. Inventory control is an extremely important component of the ____________________ distribution system. Since ____________________ -holding costs are estimated at 25 percent per year, it is important that the level of ____________________ be closely controlled.

physical
inventory
inventory

104. The economic order quantity (EOQ) model is an important technique in inventory control. The ____________________ model emphasizes the trade-off between inventory-holding costs and costs involved in placing an order to determine the optimum order quantity of each product.

EOQ

105. Customer service standards serve as a criterion under which the physical distribution manager must operate. ____________________ service standards are the statements of the quality of service that the firm's ____________________ will receive. The firm must decide if a given level of customer ____________________ is worth its cost.

customer
customers
service

106. The handling of materials is one area where increased efficiency can greatly help a firm reach its objectives. Two important innovations have recently been developed in the area of ____________________.

materials
handling

107. One innovation is called unitizing, which is the practice of combining as many packages as practical into one load that can be handled by modern equipment. This is done by using pallets and special binding procedures. ____________________ requires less labor per unit, speeds movement, and reduces theft and damage.

unitizing

108. Containerization is the other innovation. By combining several unitized loads into one container, the shipment is easily transferred from one transport mode to another. This is the principal advantage of ____________________.

containerization

109. The increase in international trade has made international ____________________ distribution an important part of the physical distribution activities of many firms.

physical

110. A major problem in ______________ physical distribution is the large amount of paperwork involved. ______________ has grown to the point where many firms subcontract, using a foreign freight-forwarder to handle the task.

international

paperwork

ASSIGNMENTS

1. For each of the goods described below, indicate the degree of market exposure you would recommend. Then, by an arrow diagram, (manufacturer → retailer → consumer) indicate which channel you would use and why you would use it. Finally, write a statement describing the services you would expect channel middlemen to provide.

(a) A line of high-quality plastic dinnerware exposure
arrow diagram
statement:

(b) A line of medium-priced campers exposure
arrow diagram
statement:

(c) A line of low-priced hand tools exposure
arrow diagram
statement:

(d) Bird seed exposure
arrow diagram
statement:

(e) A line of high-quality, high-priced stationery exposure
arrow diagram
statement:

(f) A line of high-quality precision hoses and couplings exposure
arrow diagram
statement:

2. What factors would favor the choice of the following channels?
   (a) Air travel: Channel from the transportation mode through travel agents to consumer.
      1) Consumer factors

      2) Characteristics of the product

      3) Characteristics of the firm

      4) Environmental considerations

   (b) Frozen turkeys: Channel from processor to wholesaler to retailer.
      1) Consumer factors

      2) Characteristics of the product

      3) Characteristics of the firm

      4) Environmental considerations

   (c) Classroom chairs: Channel from manufacturer direct to university.
      1) Consumer factors

      2) Characteristics of the product

      3) Characteristics of the firm

      4) Environmental considerations

3. Although your text concentrates on the marketing channels for goods, services must also be distributed. Describe the proper marketing channels for the following services. Defend your choices clearly and briefly.
   (a) Health insurance

   (b) Rock concerts

   (c) Income tax preparation service

   (d) Industrial janitorial service

4. (a) Using a map of a city near your campus, carefully outline the location of every planned shopping center.
   (b) Visit a planned shopping area and draw a map showing the location of each retail store in the center. Show the parking areas and walkways between buildings. Label each store in the center by type; for example, hardware, department, and so on.

(c) Observe the people shopping in the center and in the space provided write a description of the average shopper. Who is the shopping center's target customer?

5. Using a map of a city in your area, plot the location of the following retail stores. Is there a pattern to the location of each type of store? Write a brief statement explaining the pattern. (Use the yellow pages of the telephone directory to find the retailers in the various categories.)

(a) Florists

(b) Drug stores

(c) Furniture stores

6. Using a map of a city in your area, plot the location of the following wholesalers. In the space provided, write a brief statement explaining the pattern you find. (Use the yellow pages of the telephone directory to identify wholesalers in the various categories.)

(a) Plumbing fixtures and supplies

(b) Meat wholesalers

(c) Photographic equipment and supplies

(d) Grocery wholesalers

7. From the firms in a city in your area, identify one that would be classified as

   (a) A rack jobber

   (b) A manufacturers' agent

   (c) A broker

   (d) A full-function merchant wholesaler

   (e) A limited-function merchant wholesaler

   (f) A department store

   (g) A discount store

   (h) A chain store

8. Visit a medium or large-sized manufacturer and discuss its physical distribution system with the manager. Obtain information that will answer the following questions.

   (a) Where is the responsibility for physical distribution functions located within the firm? Draw an organization chart showing the location of the following functions: transportation, inplant warehousing, field warehousing, inventory control, order processing, and materials handling. (Be certain to include the title of each manager responsible for a physical distribution function.)

(b) Is the authority to make decisions concerning physical distribution centralized or decentralized? Defend your answer.

(c) Does the company believe its physical distribution functions can be improved? If the answer is yes, where does it believe improvement can be made?

9. Visit a company-owned warehouse and observe the materials-handling and order-processing systems. Obtain the information necessary to answer the following questions.

   (a) Draw a map illustrating the various loading and storage areas and routes used to transfer materials. Use different-colored arrows to indicate the flow of traffic to and from storage and loading areas.

(b) Does the warehouse use a computerized order-processing system? Describe the order-receiving and processing systems. On the average, how much time passes between the moment an order is received and when it is sent?

(c) Describe the materials-handling system. Is it automated?

10. Using a map of a city located near your campus, clearly mark all transportation companies found in the yellow pages of the telephone book. Use the following identification markings.

Railroad freight depots	*R*
Motor freight office	*T*
Water carrier terminals	*W*
Pipeline terminals	*P*
Air freight offices	*A*
Supplemental carriers	*S*

11. Go to the library and find a recent issue of the *Journal of Marketing.* Turn to the "Marketing Abstract" section and check for articles on subjects within the area of physical distribution. They are likely to be found under several subheadings, so review the section thoroughly. Select one article, find the publication in which it appears, and read the article from beginning to end. Then answer the following questions.

(a) Title of article

Name of author(s)

Name and date of publication

(b) What is the author's purpose in writing this article?

(c) What are the important findings or conclusions presented in the article?

(d) How do the subject and content of the article relate to the material presented in the chapter on physical distribution in your text?

CASELETS

1. Selecting a New Marketing Channel

Flotsom Boat Company was founded in 1956. The firm specializes in the manufacture and sale of twenty to thirty-four-foot pleasure craft designed specifically for saltwater boating. Since its founding, Flotsom sales and profits have increased smoothly during periods of economic growth and remained stable during periods of economic downturn. Recently, however, John Sluggo, sales manager for Flotsom, has been under pressure from Arbie Flotsom, the company president, to increase sales and profits. John believes this can best be done through Flotsom's marketing channels. After analyzing his firm's distribution pattern, John has come to the conclusion that increased sales within the company's only distributors, marinas, is unlikely.

An additional marketing channel for Flotsom has been suggested by Harvey Verekema III, a volume used-car dealer in a major west coast city. Harvey wants to sell Flotsom boats on his used-car lots, because "for many middle-class customers the choice is between a second car and a boat." Harvey has pledged to promote Flotsom boats aggressively and, in return for an exclusive dealership, will not carry any competing line of boats.

John realizes that marketing channels do change over time and he is interested in experimenting with new channel arrangements. Perhaps this new channel would increase sales and profits for Flotsom.

QUESTIONS

1. What consumer, product, firm, and environmental factors are important in making this decision?
2. What steps should be included in the selection of a new marketing channel?
3. Should John accept Harvey's offer?

2. Joining a Voluntary Chain

Harlow Hurrdle, owner and operator of Hurrdle Mart, a medium-sized supermarket located in a growing midwestern city of twelve thousand, has enjoyed fifteen years of successful operation. Recently, however, his visions of an uncomplicated future were disrupted when Super-Looper, a giant, nationwide, discount supermarket chain, announced plans to build a supermarket in a new shopping center located at the southern edge of the city.

Super-Looper is an efficient chain that sells on a high-volume, low-margin basis. Not only does Super-Looper sell national brand merchandise at low prices, it also has an excellent house brand, S-L Deluxe. The house brand is a fast-selling line of food products that is always priced a few cents below national brands.

Harlow realizes that Hurrdle Mart cannot compete on a price basis. He is hoping, however, that the fine personal service and excellent reputation of his store will keep his customers from leaving to shop at the new Super-Looper store.

Sid Sad, the general manager of Upper-Middle State Wholesalers, Incorporated, has proposed that Harlow join with his organization. Sid pointed out that this organization, a voluntary chain consisting of thirty-five independent supermarkets, can buy in quantity and obtain discounts similar to those of Super-Looper. In addition, his organization has a brand line of goods that is comparable in price and quality to S-L Deluxe. Sid stated, "If you were to join with us, you could compete with Super-Looper in all ways."

QUESTIONS

1. What benefits can a voluntary chain provide a retailer?
2. Should Harlow accept Sid's invitation to join Upper-Middle State Wholesalers, Incorporated?

3. Locating in a New Shopping Center

Kurtbeau, a medium-priced department store, is located in the downtown shopping area of a city of three hundred thousand. Five years ago one of its two major competitors closed its downtown store and moved to a large suburban shopping center that was the first center built in the area.

A week ago Kurtbeau was approached by Lars Flash, a successful shopping center developer known throughout the west. Lars is planning a new, medium-sized shopping center that will be built at the opposite edge of town from the larger existing center. The new center will contain a department store (possibly Kurtbeau), a grocery store, a hardware store, a variety store, a drug store, a discount department store, a bank, and about thirty specialty stores. Lars has asked Kurtbeau to be the department store; however, it is understood that if Kurtbeau does not accept, the remaining downtown competitor will probably build a branch store in the center.

Some officers of Kurtbeau would like to accept the offer Lars has made and establish a branch store in the new center. If, however, the branch is not profitable within four years, the company will be in financial difficulty. Other executives suggest quitting the downtown location and moving to the shopping center. However, Kurtbeau executives are not in agreement about the future of the downtown business area. For example, the federal government is planning a major office complex downtown and there is talk of a large, New York-based firm moving to the downtown area.

A major drawback to the shopping center location is the inclusion of a discount department store. Kurtbeau's executives feel there would be great competition from the discounter. Since Kurtbeau offers greater service and repair facilities for appliances, it cannot match the low prices of the minimum-service discount operation. Lars, however, is definite about his decision to include the discount department store.

QUESTION

1. What do you recommend Kurtbeau do in this situation?

4. Changing a Physical Distribution System

Middle and Frown Company, manufacturers of swine-feeding equipment sold through dealers, is considering changing its distribution system. Currently, each dealer maintains a small inventory of one or possibly two of the bulky feeder and storage units. Because the feeder-storage units must be constructed by the company, it maintains four regional warehouses at which the final assembly is completed. Since business is seasonal, the firm has always used common carriers to transport the units from the main plant to the regional warehouses and from warehouses to dealers.

However, there have been problems with this system. Service has been poor at times. Some deliveries have been late and others damaged. Fran Tarkio, marketing manager for Middle and Frown Company, has been searching for alternatives that will decrease dealer complaints and if possible, reduce physical distribution expense. Middle and Frown Company has called on you for your advice.

QUESTIONS

1. What alternative transportation arrangement would you suggest Middle and Frown Company consider? Should they buy or lease their own trucks? Should they use a contract carrier? Could Middle and Frown Company benefit from the use of some form of intermodal transportation?
2. What do you think of Middle and Frown Company's assembly and storage warehouses? Is there a better way to provide for storage and assembly?

5. Improving Customer Satisfaction

Mullhullen Textbook Company publishes college textbooks and sells them in Canada and the United States. Textbook orders are received from bookstores serving the various campuses as soon as professors place orders for their courses. All orders are filled from the company plant located in Duckabush, Washington.

Every term a number of professors are late in ordering books. This creates a rush of activity at the beginning of each term. Recently, the number of late orders has been growing, and as a consequence, delivery of texts for some classes has been as late as two weeks after the term has begun. Although complaints from professors and students have risen, the management of Mullhullen sees no way to solve the problem as long as professors continue to place orders so late.

QUESTIONS

1. What changes would you recommend be made in Mullhullen's distribution system?
2. Should Mullhullen attempt to advise professors to order early? Can company salesmen obtain accurate order estimates? In other words, can the order-processing system be improved?

Part Six
PROMOTIONAL STRATEGY

Promotion, the third variable in the marketing mix, is the subject of this part. Promotion is one of the most dynamic yet one of the most severely criticized areas in marketing. This part provides an introduction to the area of promotion.

Promotion can be defined as the marketing function of informing, persuading, and influencing the consumer's purchase decision. It consists of three basic elements: personal selling, nonpersonal selling (including advertising and sales promotion), and public relations. Effective promotional strategy requires that there be a proper mix of the elements of promotion as influenced by the type of good, value of the product, and time period involved. One of the most important tasks facing a marketing manager is the integration of the promotional plan into the overall marketing plan.

There are five basic objectives of promotion:

1. Provide information
2. Stimulate demand
3. Differentiate the product
4. Accentuate the value of the product
5. Stabilize sales.

A firm's promotional strategy is based upon the implementation of one or more of these objectives.

Promotional objectives are achieved through a promotional budget. The traditional methods of allocating a promotional budget include (1) percentage of sales, (2) fixed sum per unit, (3) meet competition, and (4) task-objective method.

Personal selling and public relations are two important parts of a firm's promotional strategy. This part examines their employment in contemporary marketing.

A brief historical review of personal selling is presented to show how selling has evolved from the Yankee peddler to the professional salesman of today. The three basic types of selling tasks—order receiving, creative selling, and missionary selling—are described to provide insight into different types of sales activities. Then, the actual steps involved in the sales process are given to ensure a thorough understanding of successful selling. These steps can be identified as

1. Prospecting and qualifying
2. Approach
3. Presentation
4. Demonstration
5. Handling objections
6. Closing
7. Follow-up.

Attention is then focused on the sales manager and his job. A manager must successfully perform several functions to increase the effectiveness of the promotional program:

1. Recruiting and selection
2. Training
3. Organization
4. Supervision
5. Compensation
6. Evaluation and control.

Public relations activities are often used to supplement other variables in the marketing mix. *Public relations* refers to the firm's communications and relationships with its various publics, including customers, suppliers, stockholders, employees, the government, and the society in which it operates. *Publicity* concerning a company's products or services is often used to supplement other promotional efforts.

Nonpersonal selling includes advertising and sales promotion. *Advertising*, which can be defined as a nonpersonal sales presentation usually directed to a large number of potential customers, is an important part of modern business. The two basic types of advertising—*product* and *institutional*—can be further classified into informative, persuasive, and reminder types. The classification is a function of the task that is performed.

Advertising-media decisions involve three basic steps:

1. Determine the audience to be reached.
2. Determine the type of medium to be employed.
3. Select the specific medium for the task.

Sales promotion applies to assorted, nonrecurrent, and somewhat extraordinary nonpersonal selling efforts. There are six basic types of sales promotion: (1) point-of-purchase advertising, (2) specialty advertising, (3) trade shows, (4) samples, coupons, and premiums, (5) contests, and (6) trading stamps.

Sales promotion techniques are used to accomplish four fundamental tasks:

1. Sales promotion objectives should relate to overall marketing and promotion objectives.
2. Sales promotion techniques should be used to supplement selling and advertising efforts.
3. The techniques should attract attention among those people they are intended to influence.
4. A sales promotion should *request* an order.

PROGRAMMED REVIEW

1. *Promotion* is another variable the marketing manager has to work with in developing a marketing mix. The function of informing, persuading, and influencing the consumer's purchase decision is called PROMOTION ________.

promotion

2. Promotional strategy is closely related to communications. Communications is the transmission of a message from a sender to a receiver. In marketing, the messages deal with buyer-seller relationships and are called marketing COMMUNICATIONS.

communications

3. The communications process can be represented by the following diagram.

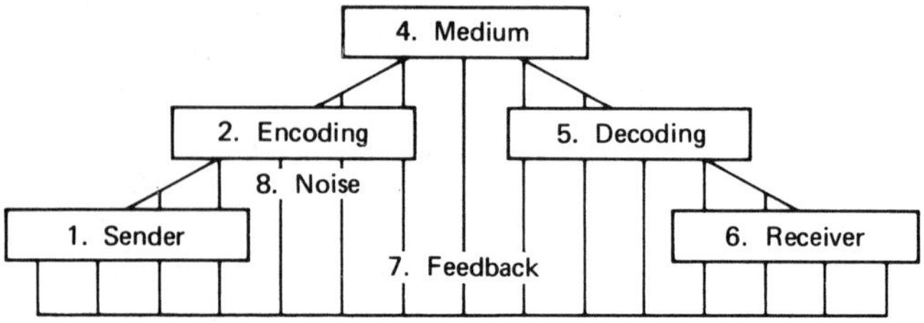

For each of the statements given below, match the element of the communications process with the statement that best describes that element.

1. sender
2. encoding
3. message
4. medium
5. decoding
6. receiver
7. feedback
8. noise

7 (a) Marketing and/or field sales reports that inform the manager about consumer decisions.
1 (b) The source of marketing communications.
3 (c) The written, oral, and/or pictorial elements that convey meaning to consumers.
6 (d) The audience or group to be communicated with.
2 (e) Translating a message into understandable form.
8 (f) Interference in the communication process, perhaps a competing message.
5 (g) The receiver's interpretation of the message.
4 (h) The communications vehicle used to transmit the message.

7 (a)
1 (b)
3 (c)
6 (d)
2 (e)
8 (f)
5 (g)
4 (h)

4. The marketer may communicate with consumers in three basic ways: through *personal selling, nonpersonal selling,* and *publicity.* The three basic elements of promotion are PERSONAL SELLING, NON-PERSONAL SELLING, and PUBLICITY.

personal selling
nonpersonal selling
publicity

5. Personal selling can be defined as a seller's promotional presentation conducted on a person-to-person basis with the buyer. A seller's promotional presentation conducted on a person-to-person basis with the buyer is called PERSONAL SELLING.

personal selling

6. Nonpersonal selling is divided into two categories: (1) advertising and (2) sales promotion. Advertising is the nonpersonal presentation of goods and services to a large audience. Sales promotion involves nonrepetitive, one-time communications efforts. Advertising and sales promotion are two categories of NON-PERSONAL SELLING.

nonpersonal selling

7. Public relations refers to a firm's communications and relationships with its various "publics." These communications efforts are usually referred to as

publicity. A firm's communications efforts with its various "publics" are referred to as PUBLICITY (PUBLIC RELATIONS).

publicity

8. The decision to emphasize personal or nonpersonal promotional presentations depends primarily on two factors: the *type of good* and the *relative value of the product.* What are the two major factors that influence the decision to emphasize personal or nonpersonal promotional presentations?

(a) TYPE OF GOODS

(b) RELETIVE VALUES OF THE PRODUCT

(a) type of good
(b) relative value of the product

9. The promotional mixes for industrial goods of high value usually emphasize personal selling. PERSONAL SELLING is usually emphasized in the promotional mixes of industrial goods of high value.

personal selling

10. More emphasis is placed on advertising for industrial goods of low value. In industrial markets for products with relatively low value, such as industrial supplies, the importance of ADVERTISING in the promotional mix is increased.

advertising

11. For low-value consumer goods, such as chewing gum, soft drinks, and snack foods, advertising is the only feasible means of promotion. Promotional mixes for low-value consumer goods tend to emphasize ADVERTISING ________.

advertising

12. Personal selling plays a larger role in the promotion of higher-priced consumer goods. As the value of consumer goods increases, PERSONAL SELLING plays a larger role in their promotion.

personal selling

13. The promotional strategy used by a firm should be designed to accomplish clearly defined promotional objectives. If a firm is to determine the effectiveness of its promotional strategy, it must have clearly defined PROMOTIONAL OBJECTIVES.

promotional objectives

14. There are many possible promotional objectives a firm might try to accomplish. Generally, however, the following can be considered objectives of promotion: *provide information, stimulate demand, product differentiation, accentuate the value of the product*, and *stabilize sales.* For each of the statements given below, fill in the objective of promotion described by that statement.

(a) The firm uses promotion to shift its demand curve and increase sales. The objective of this type of promotion is to STIMULATE DEMAND.

(b) A company uses promotion to show customers that its product is different from competing products. The objective is PRODUCT DIFFERENTIATION.

(c) Promotion can provide more possession utility to buyers and increase the value of ownership. The objective is to ACCENTUATE THE VAL OF THE PRODUCT.

(d) When a company uses promotion to tell potential consumers about the nature of a product or service and where it can be acquired, the objective is to PROVIDE INFORMATION to consumers.

(e) When a firm uses promotion to "even out" the sales of the product, it is trying to STABILIZE SALES.

(a) stimulate demand

(b) product differentiation

(c) accentuate the value of the product

(d) provide information

(e) stabilize sales

15. Management must decide how much it will spend in promoting its products. This is referred to as *budgeting for promotion.* When management determines how much to spend on promotion, it is involved in BUDGETING FOR PROMOTION.

budgeting for promotion

16. There are four methods used to budget for promotional expenditures: (1) *percentage of sales*, (2) *fixed sum per unit*, (3) *meet competition*, and (4) *task-objective method.* List the four methods used to budget for promotional expenditures.

(a) PERCENTAGE OF SALES

(b) FIXED SUM PER UNIT

(c) MEET COMPETITION

(d) TASK OBJECTIVE

(a) percentage of sales

(b) fixed sum per unit

(c) meet competition

(d) task-objective method

17. An important task that must be accomplished for effective communications is *integrating the promotional plan.* To ensure that the elements of promotion are coordinated, management must concern itself with INTEGRATE THE PROM. PLAN.

integrating the promotional plan

18. This, in turn, is a twofold problem: (1) the elements of the promotional strategy must be coordinated—the proper *promotional mix* must be

determined—and (2) the promotional mix must be appropriate for the rest of the marketing mix; that is, it must be an integral part of the *total marketing program.* To develop an effective communications system, a firm must have a coordinated __PROMOTIONAL MIX__ which is an integral part of a __TOTAL MKTG PROG.__

promotional mix

total marketing program

19. Personal selling involves face to face presentation of a firm's promotional messages. Presentation of a firm's promotional efforts through face to face relationships is referred to as __PERSONAL SELLING__.

personal selling

20. American salesmanship can be traced to the Yankee peddlers in the late seventeenth century. They sold their wares to settlers of the hinterlands. The early American salesmen sold their wares to settlers and were called __YANKEE PEDDLERS__.

Yankee peddlers

21. As population densities increased, some of these Yankee peddlers developed retail stores to serve local customers. These retailers, along with others who had established retail shops, made frequent trips to central trade areas to buy merchandise from suppliers. The suppliers had salesmen in their wholesale outlets who were called drummers. The drummers later began to travel in different areas and call on the retailers at their places of business. The suppliers' salesmen who traveled around the country calling on retailers were known as __DRUMMERS__.

drummers

22. These drummers, sometimes referred to simply as traveling salesmen, were the forerunners of today's professional salesmen. The sales job has become a professional occupation and the modern salesman can be accurately described as a __PROFESSIONAL SALESMAN__.

professional salesman

23. Sales personnel have become consultants to buyers and are concerned with performing three basic sales tasks: *order receiving, creative selling*, and *missionary selling.* The three basic sales tasks are

(a) __ORDER RECEIVING__

(b) __CREATIVE SELLING__

(c) __MISSIONARY SELLING__

(a) order receiving

(b) creative selling

(c) missionary selling

24. While most sales jobs require the performance of all three tasks, we can use these tasks for classifying a sales job on the basis of the primary selling task performed. Order receiving is part of most selling jobs and becomes primary where needs can be readily identified. A soft drink route salesman who simply replenishes a grocer's stock of beverages would be primarily concerned with performing the task of __ORDER RECEIVING__.

order receiving

25. Creative selling characterizes purchases involving considerable analytical decision making on the part of the purchaser. A manufacturer's salesman

who is trying to convince a retailer to carry his company's line of appliances would be involved in CREATIVE SELLING.

creative selling

26. Missionary selling is an indirect type of selling. Missionary selling involves selling either the good will of a company or offering technical and operational assistance to buyers. A manufacturer's salesman who aids wholesalers in locating prospective customers for his company's products would be involved in MISSIONARY SELLING.

missionary selling

27. There is one task that all salesmen are expected to perform—providing sales intelligence to the marketing organization. Every salesman is usually expected to carry out the task of PROVIDING SALES INTELLIGENCE to his firm.

providing sales intelligence

28. Selling is not an easy job. Several steps must be accomplished for a salesman to successfully complete the selling process. The first step in the selling process is prospecting and qualifying. Prospecting means seeking out potential customers while qualifying involves determining the suitability of the product for a potential customer. The first step in the selling process is called PROSPECTING and QUALIFYING ________.

prospecting

qualifying

29. Once a salesman has identified a bona fide prospect, he is ready for the second step in the sales process, the approach. The second step in the sales process involves meeting and establishing rapport with the prospective customer. This step is called the APPROACH.

approach

30. The next step in the process involves the actual sales presentation of the product or service. When the salesman begins to inform the potential customer of the product and/or services offered by his company, he is giving his sales PRESENTATION.

presentation

31. For many products, a demonstration of the product in use is critical in a sales presentation. A car salesman usually takes a prospective buyer for a ride in the automobile being considered. This is an example of a DEMONSTRATION of the product.

demonstration

32. The fifth step in the selling process involves handling objections of buyers. When the salesman attempts to answer questions and charges made by a prospect, he is said to be HANDLING OBJECTIONS.

handling objections

33. A salesman who has successfully handled the objections raised by a prospect is ready to start closing the sale. CLOSING the sale means getting the order from a customer.

closing

34. The final step in the selling process is the follow-up. This concerns the postsales activities that often determine whether a person will be a repeat customer. If a salesman contacts a buyer to determine his satisfaction with

the purchase, he is completing the step referred to as the sales FOLLOW-UP.

follow-up

35. Contemporary selling requires that management effort be exerted in managing the activities of the sales force. The manager charged with this responsibility usually has the title of sales manager. Managing the activities of the sales force is the responsibility of the SALES MANAGER ____.

sales manager

36. To fulfill his responsibilities, a sales manager must perform six basic managerial functions successfully. These include (1) *recruiting* and *selection*, (2) *training*, (3) *organization*, (4) *supervision*, (5) *compensation*, and (6) *evaluation* and *control*. Match the managerial functions given below with the statement that best describes a particular function.

1. Recruiting and selection
2. Training
3. Organization
4. Supervision
5. Compensation
6. Evaluation and control

2 (a) This function involves teaching the salesman about the company and the product he is to sell. It also provides the information he needs to perform his selling tasks.

3 (b) This involves positioning the various activities of the sales department into an effective structure.

1 (c) To complete this function, the sales manager must locate and hire good personnel.

4 (d) This function concerns communicating with the salesman and overseeing his activities to ensure that sales goals are reached.

6 (e) The manager must determine if the goals of the organization are being met and also take whatever action is needed to align the efforts of the sales force with these goals.

5 (f) To accomplish this function, the manager must develop a plan to provide salesmen with adequate income for their work.

2 (a)
3 (b)
1 (c)
4 (d)
6 (e)
5 (f)

37. A third element of promotion is public relations. Public relations is concerned with communications and relationships between the firm and its various publics. Communications and relationships between a firm and its customers, suppliers, stockholders, employees, government, and the society in which it operates are referred to as a firm's PUBLIC RELATIONS ____.

public relations

38. Publicity is the aspect of public relations that is directly related to promoting a company's products or services. Informative public relations

designed to acquaint the general public with a product's characteristics and advantages is called PUBLICITY.

publicity

39. Publicity can be a valuable *supplement* to a firm's other promotional activities. Several years ago, a large oil company changed its name and this made the headlines of most national news media. This publicity helped inform potential customers of the company's new name and therefore was a valuable SUPPLEMENT to the firm's other promotional activities.

supplement

40. Public relations should be considered an integral part of a promotional strategy. Although difficult to actually measure, PUBLIC RELATIONS can make a significant contribution to a firm's promotional strategy.

public relations

41. Today's widespread markets make it necessary for most consumer goods companies to rely on nonpersonal mass selling—advertising and sales promotion. Advertising can be defined as a nonpersonal sales presentation usually directed toward a large number of potential customers. The nonpersonal sales presentations of a firm and its products aimed at a large number of potential customers are referred to as ADVERTISING.

advertising

42. For advertising to be effective, it must seek to accomplish certain objectives. The general objectives of advertising are to inform, persuade, and remind potential customers of the firm and its products. The general advertising objectives are to INFORM, PERSUAOE, and REMIND potential customers of the firm and its products.

inform
persuade
remind

43. For measurable effectiveness, more specific advertising objectives are needed. For example, rather than simply stating that advertising should inform potential customers of a product, a more specific advertising objective would be to increase consumer knowledge of where the product can be purchased, particular product features, and uses of the product. The use of SPECIFIC ADV. GOALS will bring a firm closer to its sales goals than more general objectives.

specific advertising objectives

44. Essentially, there are two basic types of advertising: product and institutional. Product advertising is the nonpersonal selling of a particular good or service. The nonpersonal sales presentation of a particular good or service is called PRODUCT advertising.

product

45. Institutional advertising, by contrast, is concerned with promoting a concept, idea, philosophy, or the good will of an industry or a company. A

company that uses advertising to show that it has been an asset to a community is using INSTITUTIONAL advertising.

institutional

46. Product and institutional advertising can be divided further into informative, persuasive, and reminder categories. Match each type of advertising below with the statement that describes it.

1. informative product advertising
2. persuasive product advertising
3. reminder product advertising
4. informative institutional advertising
5. persuasive institutional advertising
6. reminder institutional advertising

2 (a) This is the competitive type of advertising that seeks to develop the demand for a particular product.

1 (b) This is sometimes called pioneering advertising since it seeks to develop the initial demand for a product.

4 (c) This type of advertising seeks to increase public knowledge of a concept, idea, or philosophy of an industry or company.

3 (d) This advertising is used in the maturity period of a product's life cycle to keep the name of the product before the public.

6 (e) This type of advertising seeks to remind the public of a company or an industry's concept, philosophy, and ideas.

5 (f) To advance the interests of a particular institution is the objective of this type of advertising.

2 (a)
1 (b)
4 (c)
3 (d)
6 (e)
5 (f)

47. One of the most vital decisions in developing an advertising strategy is the selection of the media to be employed. Media decisions involve three basic steps: (a) determine the audience we want to reach; (b) determine the type of medium to be employed; and (c) select the specific media for the task. List the three basic steps employed in media decisions.

(a) DETERMINE THE AUDIENCE

(b) DETERMINE MEDIA TO BE EMPLOYED

(c) SELECT SPECIFIC MEDIA

(a) determine the audience we want to reach

(b) determine the type of medium to be employed

(c) select the specific media for the task

48. The first step, determining the audience we want to reach, involves a reconsideration of the market target for the product. What we hope to accomplish is to maximize the likelihood of reaching potential customers with our advertising messages. The audience to be reached is the MARKET TARGET for the product.

market target

49. Once the audience has been specified, the next step is the choice of medium to be employed. We might be able to use television, magazines, direct mail, and so on to reach our market target. The choice of the vehicle used to send our advertising message is referred to as the choice of MEDIUM TO BE EMPLOYED.

medium to be employed

50. The final step involves selecting specific media. If magazines were the chosen medium, we would then have to select the specific magazines to be used. After considering the costs, effectiveness, and reader characteristics of different magazines, we would select the SPECIFIC MEDIA to carry our advertising messages.

specific media

51. The job of developing and carrying out an advertising strategy may be done by company personnel or a company may engage an advertising agency to carry out much of the work. An advertising agency is an independent firm that specializes in planning and implementing advertising campaigns for companies. A firm may use an ADVERTISING AGENCY to aid in planning and implementing its advertising.

advertising agency

52. The second type of nonpersonal selling is sales promotion. The assorted, nonrecurrent, and somewhat extraordinary nonpersonal selling efforts are called SALES PROMOTION.

sales promotion

53. Sales promotion activities can be divided into six different categories. The first type of sales promotion activity is point-of-purchase advertising. Point-of-purchase advertising involves displays and demonstrations that seek to promote the product at a time and place closely associated with the actual buying decision. The instore promotion of consumer goods is a common example of POINT OF PURCHASE ADV.

point-of-purchase advertising

54. Specialty advertising is another type of sales promotion. These specialties include calendars, pencils, pocket secretaries, and so on. Matchbooks bearing the name and address of a local drug store would also be an example of SPECIALTY ADVERTISING.

specialty advertising

55. Trade shows are used primarily to influence the institutional middlemen, or resellers, in the distribution channel. The annual furniture shows in Chicago and New York, at which furniture manufacturers display the latest styles of furniture for retail store buyers, are examples of the use of TRADE SHOWS as a sales promotion method.

trade shows

56. *Samples, coupons,* and *premiums* are often used as sales promotion techniques. For each statement below, fill in the blank to complete the description of the sales promotion technique.
   (a) SAMPLES are used to secure consumer acceptance of a product through free distribution of the product in moderate amounts.
   (b) PREMIUMS are bonus items given free with a purchase. The gift of a toothbrush with the purchase of a tube of toothpaste is a common example.
   (c) COUPONS offer a discount, usually five or ten cents, on the next purchase of the product.

(a) samples
(b) premiums
(c) coupons

57. A firm may sponsor a contest as a sales promotion technique. This is usually intended to attract additional customers by getting consumers involved in the company's contest. Asking consumers to submit short statements on why they like a product and awarding prizes for the best statements is an example of a CONTEST

contest

58. Trading stamps are a very common sales promotion technique. The consumer who saves stamps can redeem them for merchandise of his choice. Since the stamps are "traded" for merchandise, this promotional technique is called TRADING STAMPS.

trading stamps

59. The statements given below describe various sales promotion techniques. Match a method of sales promotion with each statement.

1. Point-of-purchase advertising
2. Specialty advertising
3. Trade shows, conventions, and expositions
4. Samples, coupons, and premiums
5. Contests
6. Trading stamps

2 (a) A company has its name imprinted on pens that are given to customers.
5 (b) A prize is given to the boy or girl who collects the most potato chip wrappers.
3 (c) Major publishing companies set up booths at a regional marketing meeting to show their latest textbooks.
1 (d) A consumer goods company has its salesmen set up displays in local grocery stores.

6 (e) A local filling station offers "Big Gold Stamps" to consumers who purchase gasoline.

4 (f) A cereal marketer puts a toy in each box of "Kiddie-Krunch" cereal.

2 (a)
5 (b)
3 (c)
1 (d)
6 (e)
4 (f)

60. Regardless of the exact technique employed, sales promotion attempts to accomplish four fundamental tasks: (a) relate to overall marketing and promotional objectives, (b) supplement personal selling and advertising efforts, (c) attract attention, and (d) seek to close a sale. What are the basic tasks accomplished through sales promotion?

(a) RELATE TO OVERALL MKTG & PROMOTIONAL OBJECTIVES

(b) SUPPLEMENT PERS. SELLING & ADV. EFFORTS

(c) ATTRACT ATTENTION

(d) CLOSE A SALE

(a) relate to overall marketing and promotional objectives

(b) supplement personal selling and advertising

(c) attract attention

(d) seek to close a sale

ASSIGNMENTS

1. Timing is considered an important factor when considering the development of a promotional strategy. In the text, three time periods—pretransactional, transactional, and posttransactional—were mentioned in showing the relative importance of advertising and selling as they apply to timing. List four products and tell how you might use promotion to your advantage during the posttransactional period. Be specific.

(a) Product 1—*Automobile—Send the customer a letter congratulating him on his decision to buy a Zoomo car. Remind him that Zoomo has great warranty service and give him a name and address to write to should he have any questions.*

(b) Product 2

(c) Product 3

(d) Product 4

2. According to the text, the decision to emphasize personal selling or advertising as the chief promotional channel depends primarily upon (1) the type of good and (2) the relative value of the product. Listed below are four products. State the chief promotional channel that should be used for each product in relation to the product type and relative value. Cite your reasons for the choices you make.

   (a) Bread

   (b) Over-the-counter headache remedies

   (c) A computer system

   (d) An ambulance

3. The text mentioned four methods of allocating a promotional budget: percentage of sales, fixed sum per unit, meet competition, and task-objective method. Take any product and briefly state how you might use each method in preparing your company's promotional budget.

   (a) Percentage of sales

   (b) Fixed sum per unit

   (c) Meet competition

   (d) Task-objective method

4. Two promotional strategies were mentioned in the text: pushing and pulling. Briefly explain what factors might influence a marketing manager's decision to choose one or the other for his product.

   (a) Pushing

   (b) Pulling

5. A prospect's objections can actually be an aid in selling the product. Specify a consumer product; list two objections a consumer might have to purchasing it; give possible replies to the objections; and state how this process may have helped in selling the product.

(a) Objection—"I don't like the seats in this model."
Reply—"*We offer a variety of interiors that includes bench seats and split-bench seats.*"
How it helped—*The objection led to a discussion of the available interiors, one of which might interest the buyer.*

(b) Objection

Reply

How it helped

6. A sale cannot be made without prospects. For the four products listed below, state what sources you might use to seek out prospects.

(a) Life insurance

(b) Children's books (door-to-door sales)

(c) Homes

(d) Automobiles

7. The text states that the higher the repeat sale potential for a product, the softer the approach the salesman will use and vice versa. List two products that fall in the "soft sell" category and two products that fall in the "hard sell" category and then explain why you think they fall in that category.

(a) "Soft sell"

1)

2)

(b) "Hard sell"

1)

2)

8. The text mentioned three selling tasks: (1) order receiving, (2) creative selling, and (3) missionary sales. Below are five situations requiring one or more tasks. State the primary task(s) to be performed and your reason for making the choice.

(a) A bread salesman calls on one of the grocery stores on his route and finds it is short of hamburger buns.

Task(s)

Reason

(b) An art-supplies salesman calls on a college bookstore to inform the manager of a new, revolutionary type of drawing paper.

Task(s)

Reason

(c) A sales representative for a computer data-processing company calls on the purchasing committee of a chain of department stores to discuss the type of information system they need.

Task(s)

Reason

(d) The salesman for the computer data-processing company calls back on the personnel involved with the equipment to help solve any problems they might have with the equipment.

Task(s)

Reason

(e) A salesman in the fleet-sales division of an automobile dealer sells a fleet of automobiles to a taxicab company.

Task(s)

Reason

9. Search current magazines and newspapers for two examples of publicity involving a firm and then answer the following questions.

(a) Example 1
Nature of publicity (describe briefly)

What will be the probable effect of this publicity on the company's image?

(b) Example 2
Nature of publicity (describe briefly)

What will be the probable effect of this publicity on the company's image?

10. Select four examples of current institutional advertising from a magazine. Tell which category—informative, persuasive, or reminder—each belongs in and why.

(a) Example

Category

Why

(b) Example

Category

Why

(c) Example

Category

Why

(d) Example

Category

Why

11. According to our text, a sales promotion should request an order. List two point-of-purchase displays and two coupons you have seen recently and tell how each attempted to "close the sale."

(a) Point-of-purchase
Display

How

Display

How

(b) Coupon
Coupon #1

How

Coupon #2

How

12. Some products are more effectively advertised through one medium than another. For each medium given below, list a product or products frequently advertised through that medium. Then explain why you think that medium is commonly used for the product you listed.

(a) Newspapers
Product—*Food products*
Why—*Housewives can compare prices from the ads and they can take the newspaper with them when shopping.*

(b) Magazines

Product

Why

(c) Television

Product

Why

(d) Radio

Product

Why

(e) Direct mail

Product

Why

(f) Outdoor

Product

Why

13. The text listed various communications goals for advertising. Cut out any three ads from a magazine to turn in. Tell which of the goals you feel each accomplished and how. (One advertisement may accomplish more than one goal.)

(a) Advertisement #1
Goals accomplished

How

(b) Advertisement #2
Goals accomplished

How

(c) Advertisement #3
Goals accomplished

How

CASELETS

1. The Klinker Toy Company

The children's toy industry had recently come under attack from consumers for what the consumers feel are unfair and misleading advertising campaigns directed at their children. A few of the complaints are

1. The toys do not perform as they are shown to in the advertising.
2. The child is led to believe that if he has the toy, all of the other children will become his friends.
3. The advertising is directed toward the child rather than the adult, who must make the purchase, and the child experiences great disappointment when he finds out he cannot have the toy.

The Klinker Toy Company has begun to feel the pressure from consumers and honestly wants to remedy the situation. It has hired the Tom Lee advertising agency to assist it in coming up with a solution.

QUESTION

1. How could the advertising agency help Klinker overcome the problem using both advertising and public relations? Be specific.

2. The Ligon Manufacturing Company

The Ligon Manufacturing Company, located in central Texas, manufactures hobby equipment in lot form. Sales over the past three years have leveled off while expenses have increased. Ligon has been a leader in its industry in developing new hobby products, but sales remain unchanged.

In previous years, Ligon has used the percentage of sales method in allocating its promotional budget. The marketing manager, John Gregory, feels that Ligon's method of allocation may be a prime factor causing static sales.

QUESTION

1. From Gregory's viewpoint, what could Ligon do to help remedy this situation? What changes would your solution entail? If necessary, use figures to illustrate your answer.

3. The ABC Can Company

The ABC Can Company is a manufacturer of aluminum and steel cans which it supplies to the beer, soft drink, and canned goods industries. John Brown, ABC's president, has been concerned over the recent upsurge in protest over the use of nonrecyclable steel cans, and he wants to know if perhaps some of the investment ABC has in steel cans might be applied to greater advantage in aluminum cans.

Below are some excerpts from the income statement and balance sheet of ABC for the last three years.

	1971		1972		1973	
	ALUMINUM CANS	STEEL CANS	ALUMINUM CANS	STEEL CANS	ALUMINUM CANS	STEEL CANS
Investment	250,000	500,000	250,000	500,000	250,000	500,000
Sales	400,000	1,000,000	600,000	900,000	650,000	650,000
Net Profit	90,000	250,000	115,000	225,000	150,000	185,000

QUESTION

1. If you were the sales manager, what might you recommend if you used the ROI method of evaluation? Why?

4. The Fortrend Company

The Fortrend Company is a major producer of electrical appliances. The company's salesmen sell to wholesalers and distributors throughout the United States and Canada. Because of the nature of their selling job, the salesmen have been paid a straight salary.

Fortrend is contemplating adding a new division that will sell directly to tract home builders. This would involve a package deal in which Fortrend would furnish all the electrical appliances in the houses (for example, refrigerator, stove, water heater, dishwasher, garbage disposal, washing machine, clothes dryer, and heating and cooling systems). Some of these items will not be manufactured by Fortrend, but will still be part of the package through arrangements with other manufacturers.

One consideration in establishing the new division is the sales force. It is believed the type of salesman needed is the creative type.

QUESTION

1. What type of compensation plan might be most effective for the new division? Why?

5. The Carmo Furniture Company

The Carmo Furniture Company is a large manufacturer of household and business furniture. Carmo is known as a leader in the industry and proof of this is its product-research department which is particularly farsighted.

One year ago, Carmo developed and marketed a revolutionary type of wooden furniture. The unique features of the furniture made it scratchproof and burnproof and it never had to be waxed. Carmo had this segment of the market all to itself.

Within the last few months, several other furniture manufacturers have begun marketing furniture with all the advantages of the Carmo furniture.

For the past year, Carmo's advertising campaign has centered on informing the public of the availability of the new furniture. Carmo now feels that the basic objective of its advertising should change.

QUESTION

1. What new objective should be established? Give examples of ads that might be used to accomplish the new objective.

Part Seven
PRICING STRATEGY

Pricing is an extremely important and challenging aspect of the management of marketing. While price may be defined as the exchange value of a good or service, the determination of the offering price must consider not only the cost of providing it but also the consumer's perception of and reaction to that price.

An improper price can damage the overall marketing effort. Price interacts with many other variables such as style, quality, the nature of the market, the consumer's interest in price, and his ability to judge prices.

It is important for the firm to set pricing objectives that are compatible with overall company objectives and marketing objectives. Once pricing objectives have been determined, it is easier for the manager to price consistently over time and among the various products the firm markets.

Pricing objectives are divided into profitability, volume, and other objectives. *Profitability objectives* include *profit maximization* and *target return on investment. Volume objectives* include *sales maximization* and *market share.* Several other objectives are included in the third classification. They are (1) *social and ethical considerations*, (2) *status quo objectives*, and (3) *prestige objectives.* Many firms use multiple objectives in their pricing program, for any one objective may not guide decision makers sufficiently in this difficult task. It is necessary, however, for the marketing manager to be aware of the various objectives and to select those that can be adapted to the marketing program.

The determination of prices is not an easy task. The decision maker does not have full information about the conditions under which his products will be sold, especially the product demand. However, with a set of clear-cut, practical objectives, he will have an advantage over those of his competitors who do not have such objectives.

The approaches to basic price determination have fallen into two groups of techniques—the application of price theory and the cost-plus approach. In addition, customer, tradition, and social habit play important roles, especially for certain products and services.

An understanding of the theoretical framework for pricing found in *price theory* provides a rigorous examination of price setting in the types of market situations known to exist. It also provides a rational approach to price determination. Although there are several limitations that minimize the application of price theory, it does provide the basis for sound pricing. Thus, the application of *marginal analysis* to *pure competition*, *monopolistic competition*, *oligopoly*, and *monopoly* should be thoroughly understood. Because of the difficulty of determining demand and other limitations, price theory is difficult to apply. Much of practical pricing is based on cost-plus pricing approaches.

The *cost-plus approach* is not a complete answer to the decision maker's dilemma either, for it, too, has limitations. For example, cost may be determined in different ways; if one uses the *full-cost approach* and then adds a margin, the product may be overpriced to the consumer. The *incremental cost* approach does not guarantee a correct price either. The main problem with cost-plus approaches is that they do not adequately account for product demand. Also, cost-plus approaches usually assume a uniform cost and price relationship; yet cost is not the sole nor even the major determinant of the selling price. *Principally, cost is a floor for price.*

To improve these weaknesses in the cost-plus approach, the decision maker can use break-even analysis, flexible markups based on turnover, and a pricing process that includes consideration of nonprice factors.

Break-even analysis can aid the decision maker when choosing among several pricing alternatives. *Flexible markups* give the manager the opportunity to depart from traditional pricing practices. The *multistage approach to pricing* reminds the manager to consider many areas of potential danger, including such elements as the market target, brand image, and the marketing mix, that must be developed during the process. All three techniques can aid the perceptive manager in developing prices that give the firm a solid market offering.

Pricing strategy is the composite of industry pricing practices and company policies put to use in a given situation to attain specific pricing objectives. Pricing decisions are made within the organizational context, using accepted methods of quoting price and following prescribed policy.

Many factors influence the size and type of pricing organizations; however, the recent evolution of the marketing concept has placed the responsibility for setting and administering price in the marketing department.

Although price-quoting methods vary by industry, the use of *discounts* and *allowances* is generally accepted. *Cash*, *trade*, and *quantity* discounts, together with trade-ins, promotional, and brokerage allowances, are deductions from list price widely used to arrive at the market price. *Cash discounts* are deductions from list price for the prompt payment of the invoice. *Trade or functional discounts* are given to a buyer for performing some normally required service. Promotional allowances may also be given to the same buyer for performing a service that is not normally required. *Quantity discounts* are granted for large purchases. Trade-ins and brokerage allowances are special-situation deductions.

Transportation expense may be handled in several different ways, depending on the type of product, industry practice, and the individual firm's geographic location. Specific policies described are *f.o.b. (free on board)*, *freight absorption*, *uniform delivered price*, *zone pricing*, and *basing points.* When a price is quoted *f.o.b.*, the buyer pays all shipping charges. When following a policy of *freight absorption*, the seller pays the shipping charge by permitting the buyer to deduct his transportation expense from the bill. By quoting a *uniform delivered price*, the seller averages transportation charges and quotes a single price that includes transportation. When using this method, the buyer located close to the shipping point pays *phantom freight*, which is that portion of the bill charged for shipping services the buyer does not receive. *Zone pricing* is a modified form of uniform delivered pricing. Basing-point pricing is an industry practice that is not widely used; in several instances it has been declared illegal.

Price quoting includes *psychological aspects* because buyers often use price as a guide to decision making. Psychological considerations have led to the use of *prestige pricing* and *odd pricing.*

Pricing policies are important aids to pricing, for they interpret the intent of price objectives for recurring price situations. These policies serve as guidelines to assure consistency in pricing throughout the organization. Pricing policies are usually developed for pricing new products, price flexibility, price levels, price lines, and price promotions.

There are two basic policies for pricing a new product. *Skim-the-cream or* simply *skimming policy* is often followed when a product is quite different from existing products; competing products are not soon expected on the market; and the firm wishes to recover its research and development costs quickly. *A penetration policy* is followed when the firm wishes to capture a large share of the market quickly and develop brand loyalty.

The two basic policies concerned with *price flexibility* are *one-price* and *variable.* A one-price policy is normally used in conjunction with mass selling, while variable pricing is used when bargaining is a selling mode.

The firm should set a *relative price level* for each product. Once established, marketing and sales personnel can price consistently according to the market. A firm may price above, below, or at the prevailing market price. The choice will depend upon many factors including company, brand, and product image.

Consumer goods are often marketed within *price lines;* that is, they are priced within defined price ranges. Establishing the specific number and range for products sold increases consistency in pricing.

How price will be used in promoting the sale of a product is an important policy question. Price may be used to promote sales volume in a number of ways. For example, *loss-leader* promotions are common in retailing. Policies that specify the type and amount of *promotional pricing* serve as useful guides to the managers of retail chain stores and the sales representatives of manufacturers. Such policies also serve to prevent the firm from engaging in illegal promotional pricing practices.

The marketing manager should have a set of well-defined price policies, for if followed they assure a degree of consistency and allow pricing decisions to be delegated.

How the buyer perceives and reacts to price is an important aspect of pricing. Numerous research studies on the consumer's perception of the relationship of *price* and *quality* have been made. It has been argued that consumers have *price limits* for each product and the firm should set a price within that limit.

Pricing in special situations is an area of growing importance. These situations are negotiated prices, competitive bidding, transfer pricing, and public service pricing.

Many governmental and industrial procurement systems require *competitive bidding* or *negotiation.* These are situations that call for specialized knowledge and procedures.

With the growth of large-scale enterprise there is increased sale of products between organizational units of the same firm. Determining the proper price in these nonmarket situations is called *transfer pricing.* The problem is very important both to the buyer and the seller, for usually each is a *profit center* responsible for its own revenues and costs.

With the growth of big government has come the awareness that *public services* are marketed. Pricing, long neglected by governmental agencies, is becoming a problem. The pricing of public services is complicated by the political objectives that are often more important than market considerations.

Thus, the marketing manager must be aware of the importance of pricing to his overall marketing effort. To incorporate an effective pricing operation into his marketing mix, the manager must set policies and be aware of his market situation at all times.

PROGRAMMED REVIEW

1. Pricing is one of the most challenging aspects of marketing, for it is based on both judgment and quantitative analysis. While ____________________ is important, it is not the sole determinant in the purchase of a good or service.

price

2. ____________________ is the exchange value of a good or service. To the firm, however, prices represent the revenue to be received and therefore influence both its profits and employment of resources.

price

3. Often price is not the foremost consideration in the marketing mix because consumers are also interested in quality, service, and other nonprice factors. Nevertheless, the problem of ____________________ is still important because volume and price are related.

price

4. A firm's pricing objectives are very important to the effectiveness of its pricing operations. Pricing ____________________ should be in line with marketing and overall company objectives.

objectives

5. There are three major classifications of pricing objectives. They are profitability, volume, and other ____________________.

objectives

6. The first group of objectives, which are called ____________________ objectives, includes profit ____________________ and target return on investment.

profitability

maximization

7. Target ____________________ objectives are common for they are easier to implement and serve as useful guidelines in evaluating overall corporate activity.

return

8. Two objectives—sales maximization and market share—are called volume ________________. Using sales ________________, the firm sets a minimum floor at the point it considers the lowest acceptable profit level and then it seeks to maximize ________________.

objectives

maximization

sales

9. When using ________________ share, the firm prices to achieve a specific share of the total sales of a product. Thus, market share is expressed as a percentage of total industry sales.

market

10. Market ________________ is more easily measured and is in line with the idea of expansion and the growth of profits. Courts and the government have also found ________________ share useful in dealing with firms, since market share is an indicator of a company's strength relative to other firms.

share

market

11. The third classification includes social and ethical considerations, status quo, and prestige ________________. Social and ________________ considerations are becoming a more important part of pricing.

objectives

ethical

12. Some large companies desire to minimize pricing action. Some observers believe that stable price conditions lead to better, more personalized customer service. Thus, ________________ objectives are used by some ________________ and some industries.

status quo

firms

13. Often a firm will want to give a product a prestige image and will set ________________ goals for pricing.

prestige

14. There are two ways to look at price setting: one is price theory (theoretical price determination) and the other is cost-plus. Customers, tradition, and social habit also play a role in ________________ determination.

price

15. The theoretical approach to setting price is extremely difficult to apply in actual practice for several reasons: it is difficult to determine demand and it does not include nonprice factors. In addition, the ________________ approach is based on many assumptions that may not be true in a given ________________ situation.

theoretical

pricing

16. Using the theoretical approach, all firms are assumed to be following profit ________________ objectives. This approach also assumes that the firm is pricing in one of several specific market situations. The ________________ are pure competition, monopolistic competition, oligopoly, and monopoly.

maximization situations	17. By assuming that the firm will set prices at the point of maximum ____________________, price is determined for each market situation.
profit	18. Actual price determination tends to be based on some form of the cost- ____________________ approach. Basically, this approach is applied by adding a markup to cover unassigned costs and profit to some base ____________________ figure.
plus cost	19. Unfortunately, costs do not determine ____________________ consumers set price by their actions in the market. Cost does, however, provide a tool for analyzing the profitability of various pricing alternatives.
price	20. The two most common methods of cost-oriented ____________________ are the full-cost and incremental-cost ____________________.
pricing methods	21. There are serious limitations to cost-oriented pricing. For example, ____________________ pricing does not adequately account for product demand. Thus, some other tools are useful in price ____________________.
cost-oriented determination	22. Break-even analysis is one of the tools that can be of great benefit in pricing. ____________________ analysis allows the decision maker to compare the profit consequences of different prices.
break-even	23. Using total-revenue and total-cost projections, a point where the firm will just break even can be found. This break-even ____________________ can also be found by dividing the firm's total fixed costs by the per unit contribution to fixed ____________________.
point costs	24. To find the per ____________________ contribution to fixed costs, all you need is your selling ____________________ and average variable cost.
unit price	25. By extending a total-revenue line for each price and estimating total demand for each price, a total demand curve can be developed. The ____________________ demand curve gives the decision maker a visual presentation of estimated profit for each price.
total	26. Markup, markons, and turnover are important aids to the decision maker. A ____________________ is the amount added to the cost of an item to determine selling price. It is stated as a percentage of the selling price.
markup	27. A markon is a ____________________ expressed as a percentage of cost.

markup 28. A major problem with markup is that certain percentages tend to become traditional within an industry or for an item. One way to build flexibility into pricing is to vary ________________ with stock turnover.

markup 29. Stock ________________ is the number of times the average inventory is sold each year. For example, if average ________________ is $30,000 and sales were $300,000, then ________________ turnover is ten.

turnover
inventory
stock

30. As a guide, it is suggested that if you wish your stock ________________ to be high relative to your competition, then your ________________ should be lower than the average in your industry.

turnover
markup

31. If you are a retailer selling items similar to your competitor and you wish to move merchandise quickly and increase ________________, you should add ________________ markups than your competitor.

turnover
lower

32. Most of the methods for determining ________________ discussed so far have concentrated on the selection of a specific price rather than the process of price determination. In addition, the nonprice aspects of the price decision have not been emphasized.

price 33. The multistage approach to pricing developed by Alfred R. Oxenfeldt stresses the pricing ________________ and nonprice factors that are important to pricing.

process 34. By following the ________________ approach to pricing, a decision maker is more likely to set a ________________ that is correctly related to the other products being sold and to the marketing mix for the product.

multistage
price

35. The first stage is the selection of market targets. It is assumed that the decision maker will study these ________________ so that the price will appeal to consumers in each market target.

market targets

36. The next stage is the selection of a brand image and the third ________________ is the development of the marketing ________________. Both brand ________________ and ________________ mix should be compatible with each other and the market ________________.

stage
mix
image
marketing
target

37. Stages four and ________________ deal with policy and strategy considerations. Development of ________________ ________ policies is important for consistency in the marketing effort.

five
price

38. Within the constraints set up by the first five stages, a range of acceptable ________________ remains. By using break-even ________ ________________, cost and demand information, and good executive judgment, the price is set at the sixth ________________ ________ .

prices
analysis
stage

39. To administer a pricing program, a firm must organize human resources and develop ________________ policies.

pricing

40. Traditionally, accountants and cost clerks handled the setting of ________ ________________. With the coming of the marketing concept and the realization that the components of the marketing ________________ ________________ need to be coordinated, both ________________ ________________ and administration of price were assigned to marketing management.

prices
mix
setting

41. There are many ways in which responsibility for pricing can be assigned. In some firms, pricing ________________ are centralized; in others they are not. The organization of ________________ ________ is influenced by many factors.

decisions
pricing

42. Although the method for quoting price depends on many factors, there are certain accepted practices such as discounts, allowances, and geographic pricing practices that aid the manager in carrying out his ________________ ________________ -quoting responsibilities.

price

43. Most prices are ________________ at list price because the list is the basic price from which the final or market price is determined.

quoted

44. Discounts and allowances are deductions from ________________ ________________ price in payment for some service performed for the seller.

list

45. The common discounts are cash, trade, and quantity. ________________ ________________ discounts are given for the prompt payment of a bill.

cash

46. Trade ________________, which are also called functional discounts, are deductions from ________________ price given to channel members for performing various marketing functions.

discounts
list

47. Quantity ______ are percentage reductions from list ______ for volume purchased. There are two types of ______ discounts. The more common are called noncumulative, for they are determined by the size of each order. Cumulative ______ discounts are determined by volume purchased over a certain period of time.

discounts
price
quantity
quantity

48. Allowances are similar to ______, for they are both reductions from ______ price. The three types of ______ mentioned in the text are trade-ins, promotional allowances, and brokerage allowances.

discounts
list
allowances

49. When a seller wants to encourage a channel buyer to do something specific for him, such as advertise or engage in extra selling effort, he has to pay the buyer. Payment for these extra services is made by promotional ______.

allowances

50. A major cost consideration in marketing is transportation, which was studied in the chapter on physical ______. Since most sales involve the movement of goods, buyers and sellers must determine who is going to pay for ______.

distribution
transportation

51. There are several policies that sellers can use in handling transportation ______. They include f.o.b., freight absorption, uniform delivered price, zone pricing, and basing points.

costs

52. A price quoted f.o.b. (free on board) does not include any shipping costs. The seller simply loads the merchandise on board the carrier and from then on the ______ pays all costs. By following this policy, a seller limits his trading area, especially if ______ costs are a major cost of the delivered merchandise.

buyer
transportation

53. Sellers may elect to follow a policy of paying all transportation expenses. When using this method, which is called freight ______, the seller can quote the same price regardless of the location.

absorption

54. When using a policy of uniform delivered price, the seller ______ the same price to all buyers. Transportation costs paid by the buyer as part of the quoted ______ include an average transportation charge.

quotes
price

55. By charging all ______ an average ______ cost, the seller is, in effect, overcharging some buyers for transportation and undercharging others. Those buyers located close to the shipping point are paying in excess of the actual cost of shipping the goods. This excess charge is called phantom freight.

buyers
transportation

56. Zone ____________________ is a system of uniform delivered pricing within geographic areas. Mail order firms often use this method.

pricing

57. Since much of pricing is concerned with how the buyer perceives price, the psychological aspect of price quoting is important. ____________________ pricing includes prestige pricing and odd ____________________. Use of ____________________ pricing is believed to attract more attention to the product.

psychological
pricing
odd

58. To provide guidelines for decision makers, to assure consistency in pricing decisions, and to control pricing, firms should establish ____________________ policies.

pricing

59. Several important pricing ____________________ are discussed in the text. They include new-product pricing, price flexibility, relative price levels, price lining, and promotional prices.

policies

60. The initial price for a product is a particularly difficult task, for the ____________________ maker has very little information upon which to base his choice. However, there are two basic approaches to setting the price on a ____________________ product. The firm may follow a skimming or a penetration policy.

decision
new

61. A relatively high introductory price is set when following a skimming ____________________. The purpose is to recover research and other sunk costs rapidly. A ____________________ policy, however, attracts competition, which in turn forces the firm to ____________________ the price.

policy
skimming
lower

62. A policy of penetration pricing requires a low initial ____________________. The purpose of the low ____________________ price is to obtain a large share of the market and strong brand loyalty. Penetration prices discourage competitors from entering the market.

price
penetration

63. The degree of price flexibility allowed is another policy decision for the firm's executives. The firm may follow a one-price ____________________ or it may employ variable pricing. Retailers wishing high stock turnover and using mass-selling techniques usually follow a ____________________ policy.

policy
one-price

64. In order to price consistently, it is necessary to set policy regarding price levels. Should the firm price above, at, or below the prices set by competing firms? ____________________ should be compatible with the other components of the marketing mix and the ____________________ the company wishes to project to consumers.

price levels
image

65. Quite often companies follow the policy of price lining. This is the practice of marketing products at a limited number of price ranges. When properly done, ________________ is a practical guide for consumers. The firm should set ________________ ranges that appeal to the market segments it is attempting to serve.

price lining
price

66. Decision makers must decide to what extent price will be used to promote sales volume. ________________ price policies need to be set and integrated with the firm's marketing ________________.

promotional
mix

67. There are many different promotional ________________ practices. At the retail level, loss leaders are often used. When retailers price goods very low in order to attract customers who will probably buy other regularly priced goods, they are using ________________.

price
loss leaders

68. Price is an important indicator of quality to buyers. This is especially true when the buyer has little knowledge of the product design and manufacture. There have been a number of studies done to test the relationship of ________________ and ________________.

price
quality

69. It has been argued that consumers have price limits around which their perceptions of product ________________ vary directly with price. A price below this limit is considered too low and a ________________ above the limit is too high.

quality
price

70. Markets in which price is set by competitive bidding are growing rapidly. ________________ bidding requires knowledge of the specifications and the practice of estimating.

competitive

71. Negotiated contracts are a form of pricing that is important in industrial and governmental markets. ________________ contracts are often used when there is only one available supplier and/or the job requires extensive research and development work.

negotiated

72. With the growth of large, multidivisional organizations, the problem of transfer pricing is becoming more important. A ________________ price is the price charged for goods that are sold by one organizational unit to another. The ________________-setting problem is difficult because each unit is a profit center responsible for revenues and costs.

transfer
price

73. The pricing of public services is an emerging pricing issue. Public ________________ were traditionally priced using the full-cost approach. Recently, however, the trend has been toward the use of the incremental approach.

services 74. The multiple goals of public service units also cause difficulty. In some cases, for example, ______________ is set to discourage the use of a service rather than to set a fair or just price.

price

ASSIGNMENTS

1. Interview the marketing manager of a manufacturing or a service firm. He may be a product or division manager or the general marketing manager for his firm. After learning about the marketing operation, hand him twelve cards, each containing a policy area listed in Figure 14—1 of your text. Ask him to rank the policy areas in order of importance to his product line.

RANKING OF POLICIES GIVEN IN TEXT	RANKING OF POLICIES FOR ______________ COMPANY (PRODUCT OR SERVICE)
1.	1.
2.	2.
3.	3.
4.	4.
5.	5.
6.	6.
7.	7.
8.	8.
9.	9.
10.	10.
11.	11.
12.	12.

Are the two lists different in any important way? Write a brief statement explaining why they differ.

2. (a) Ask ten people to estimate the average retail markup on the following items. Be certain to explain what you mean by markup.

		ESTIMATED PERCENT OF MARKUP						
ACTUAL PERCENT OF MARKUP	ITEM	UNDER 20	20–39	40–59	60–79	80–99	100–120	OVER 120
	(a) Toothpaste							
	(b) Indoor-outdoor carpeting							
	(c) Luggage							
	(d) Electric toasters							
	(e) Paperback books							
	(f) Fine china dishes							
	(g) Fresh fruits and vegetables							
	(h) Food in a restaurant							

(b) Compare your findings with the average retail markups for these products. Place the average markup figures in the column to the left of the product name.

(c) What conclusions can you draw from your findings?

3. What type of pricing objective would you recommend for each of the following items? Why?

(a) A kennel specializing in collie dogs

(b) The United States Park Service in pricing use of national parks

(c) A firm manufacturing and marketing an undifferentiated line of commercial floor cleaner

(d) A city transit authority pricing bus rides

(e) A large, geographically decentralized, janitorial service bidding on government and industrial jobs

4. The Olive Company wants to use break-even analysis to determine its price for canned olives. Fixed costs for next year are $60,000. Variable costs are 50 percent of sales. Prices and estimated volume are given below.

PRICE	EXPECTED (000 OMITTED)	SALES	TOTAL REVENUE	FIXED COSTS	VARIABLE COSTS	TOTAL COSTS	PROFIT BEFORE TAXES
.23	500						
.25	490						
.28	480						
.30	450						
.33	400						

(a) Fill in the schedule.
(b) At which price are expected profits the highest?
(c) Figure the break-even point for three of the five prices.

5. Visit stores in your area and identify price lines for the following items. Give reasons for the differences you find in price lines.

(a) Women's belts

(b) Electric typewriters

(c) Manual typewriters

(d) Pen and pencil sets

(e) Movie cameras

(f) Cassette recorders

6. Carefully read your local daily newspaper for one week. Make a list of the loss leaders advertised. Include the regular price (if readily determined) and the discount price. If more than one store is advertising the same item as a loss leader, note which store advertised first.

7. Establish a zone-pricing schedule for two of the following firms. Use the outline maps of the United States and Canada shown below. Assume that the firms are located in the community in which your campus is located. Justify the zones you have set up.

   (a) A specialty mail-order house. No item sent is over three pounds.
   (b) A firm selling specialty canned vegetables and cheese packs. Weight varies from one to ten pounds. They are sold to retail stores (drug, flower, and gift shops).
   (c) Sleeping bags sold through sporting-goods stores and department stores.
   (d) A nursery selling small, young fruit trees, approximately three feet high, and shipped in bulk with wrapping around roots and soil. They are sold to commercial fruit growers and local nurseries.

8. Select an item you have recently purchased. Show the item to ten people and ask them to estimate the price. If they give you a price range, select the average price within the range and write it in the space provided. Then ask each why he or she chose that price. Do not use staple goods such as grocery or drug items whose prices are widely known.

   (a) Item description

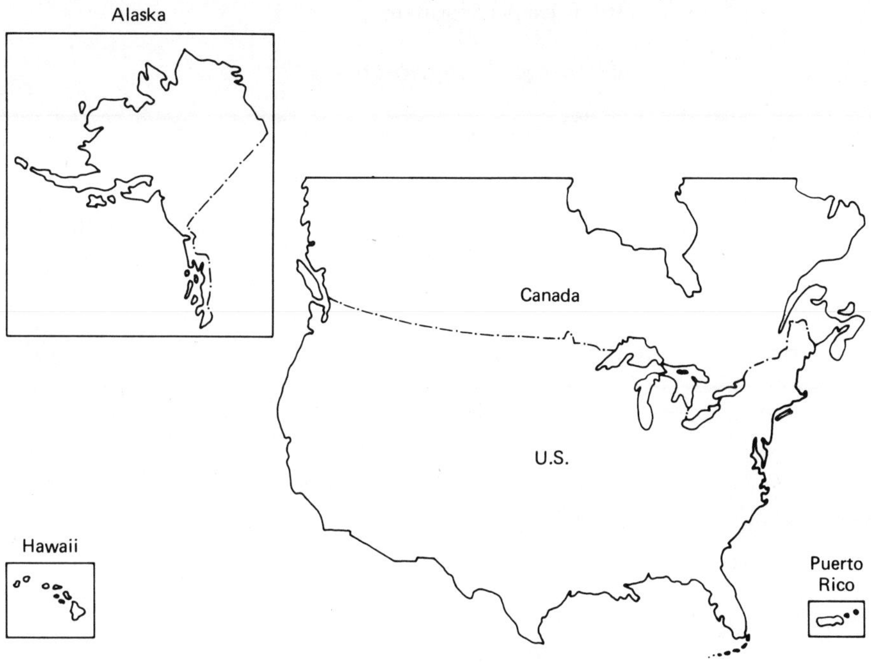
Alaska
Canada
U.S.
Hawaii
Puerto
Rico

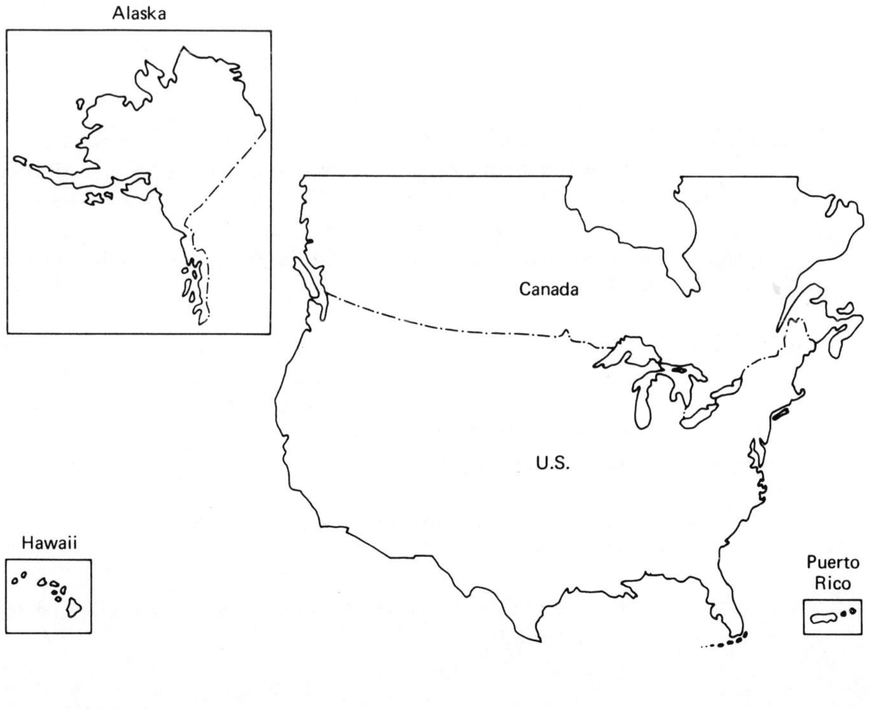
Alaska
Canada
U.S.
Hawaii
Puerto
Rico

(b) Price paid for item

(c) Range of estimated prices

Highest 1.

2.

3.

4.

5.

6.

7.

8.

9.

Lowest 10.

(d) Reasons given most often for estimated price

CASELETS

1. Setting Pricing Objectives

It is well known in Faraway County that Connie Sunky is an excellent cook. Connie has many original recipes that have won blue ribbons at the state fair. Connie is best known, however, for her delicious salad dressing.

For several years, she has been urged by retailers and friends to market her dressing. Today she borrowed $4000 from the local bank to produce and sell her product.

QUESTION

1. Assume that Connie resides in the community in which your campus is located and plans to market in a five-state region. Complete the first three steps of the multistage approach to pricing and then write the pricing objectives for Connie's product.
   (a) Market target is

   (b) Brand and company image should be

   (c) Composition of the marketing mix (especially the role price will play) should be

(d) Statement of pricing objective(s)

2. Estimating Demand

Carol Klumm, director of marketing research for Uwe Door Company, has been asked by Ron Uwe, the company president, to estimate demand after a proposed change in the firm's price level.

Uwe markets a medium-priced door purchased mainly by contractors and builders of apartment buildings and single-unit residences. Prices for labor and material have risen to the point where a change of some kind must be made. Mr. Uwe has considered a 10 percent price increase, but before announcing the change he wants to know if sales will decline drastically.

QUESTION

1. Can Carol provide a reliable estimate? How should she go about estimating demand?

3. Price Policy for a New Product

Kurt Thormillsun, a university-educated lumberjack from Ketchikan, Alaska, has developed a revolutionary new tool for harvesting trees. The product is lightweight, fast, requires little servicing, and is relatively inexpensive to operate. It is powered by a special energy cell that utilizes ultrasonic technology and must be replaced every three hundred hours of use.

Kurt estimates the average production costs for the basic tool to be $60.00 and the production costs for the energy cell to be $20.00. These estimates include both fixed and variable costs.

Kurt plans to sell the product to professional loggers, lumber companies, and anyone who uses a chain saw extensively. Production specifications call for materials and workmanship of good quality; thus, the basic tool is expected to last six years under average working conditions.

Kurt has the patent covering the process and is the only one who can manufacture and sell the basic tool and energy cell.

QUESTION

1. Should Kurt follow a skimming or a penetration policy? Why?

4. Setting Promotional Discounts

Till Company has a problem. Distributors are not promoting the company's line of hand warmers satisfactorily. Bill Swift, a bright, young M.B.A. recently hired by the firm as assistant to the director of marketing, has suggested a solution. Bill believes firmly that Till should raise its retail price, thereby increasing the amount of discount per item received by both wholesalers and retailers.

Marilyn Twill, the sales manager for Till, is very upset with young Bill's proposal. Marilyn favors the use of promotional allowances given for specific services. For example, she would use cooperative advertising and spiffs.[1]

QUESTIONS

1. What are the advantages and disadvantages of each proposal?
2. Assume that you are the director of marketing for Till Company. Which of the two alternatives would you use? Why?

---

[1] Spiffs are payments made directly to salesclerks and wholesaler salesmen and usually figured as a percentage of sales.

Part Eight

MARKETING AND SOCIETY

The successful performance of the marketing task is dependent upon persons and organizations outside the firm. *Marketing represents the firm's most constant and important contact with the environment.* It is marketing personnel, salesmen, researchers, and management who filter information from the market to the firm's decision centers. Recently, the focus of interaction has expanded beyond the channel members and consumers to include all elements of society.

Now more than ever before, marketers must keep up-to-date on environmental change. These environmental relationships, called externalities, form the basis of the important and growing awareness of societal issues. The marketing manager is vitally involved in social issues. *Not only is the manager a transmitter of environmental information to the firm, he is also a key factor in the resolution of social issues.*

The current clash between our materialistic tradition of emphasizing growth and an antimaterialistic subculture is being reflected by increased pressure on marketing from sources within the environment. These pressures will probably continue until a synthesis of the two value sets occurs.

The problem of coping with these pressures is made more complex by the lack of standards to evaluate marketing performance. Until tools for measuring social values, such as a quality of life index, are constructed and until there is agreement on the policy guidelines for the marketing manager to follow, contemporary social issues will remain a perplexing problem for marketing management.

The categorization of contemporary social issues used by your authors includes three major subjects: *consumerism*, *marketing ethics*, and *social responsibility*.

Consumerism is characterized as a protest against the abuses and malpractices of our marketing system. Some people feel that inadequacies in the marketing concept and the lack of adoption of the concept have caused the problem. It is important to note, however, that the *criticisms of the marketing system are aimed primarily at the system of competitive marketing and only secondarily at the marketing concept.* Nor are most of the criticisms new, for they can be traced back to the complaints about trading in ancient history.

The charges made against marketing in a competitive marketing system are

1. Marketing costs are too high.
2. The marketing system is inefficient.
3. Marketers are guilty of collusion and price fixing.
4. Product quality and service are poor.
5. The marketing system has produced health and safety hazards.
6. Consumers do not receive complete information.

It is important for marketing managers to be aware of these charges and of all the arguments for and against a competitive marketing system.

Much of the current interest in consumerism revolves around the rights of consumers to choose, to be heard, to be safeguarded, and to be informed. To help protect these rights, public action has included (1) passage of legislation to aid the consumer; (2) creation of additional consumer protection agencies; and (3) an expanded consumer-education program. In addition, the concepts of class-action and mass-restitution suits have been instituted.

The response of individual business firms has included (1) customer grievance channels, (2) realistic consumer advertising, (3) executive-consumer panels, (4) improved product-servicing programs, and (5) the establishment of departments to deal with consumer issues.

Marketing ethics, another of the major categories of social issues presented in your text, *is an area receiving increased attention because of the need to set standards to guide and judge the conduct of marketers.* The three basic ethical philosophies discussed are *utilitarianism*, *moral idealism*, and *intuitionism*. *Utilitarianism* looks to the consequences of an act to assess its morality. *Moral idealism* is concerned with setting a general standard of conduct or code of ethics that will serve as a standard for guiding and judging behavior. *Intuitionism* judges an act on the basis of the motive of the participants in the act.

For the individual, a *conflict* of importance sometimes occurs *between his ethic and that of the organization* in which he works. It has been suggested that marketing develop its own *professional ethic* as a basis of authority. The degree of success of this approach would depend in part upon the degree to which marketers would be indoctrinated or educated to be loyal to the ethic.

There are several areas in which ethical problems arise. They are research, product management, channel strategy, promotion, and pricing.

Social responsibility is the third contemporary social issue affecting marketing and society. While marketing ethics focus on the decisions of the individual decision maker, *social responsibility is concerned with broader issues, including the relationship between social responsibility in marketing and the profit motive and the locus for socially responsible decisions in the organization.*

There are many parties arguing different positions on each issue. Regardless of these arguments, it is a reality that marketing plays an important role in the resolution of social issues even when the decision-making power does not rest with the marketing department. This is because of marketing's position between top management and the environment. For example, although the decision to continue operating a profitable but air-polluting plant may be made by top management, it is the marketing department that must cope with the resulting complaints from interest groups. Decisions concerning ecology are particularly sensitive at this time. The marketing department is likely to be involved in resolving issues such as planned obsolescence, environmental pollution, cultural pollution, the recycling of waste materials, and the preservation of resources.

Continued efforts to resolve problems in the areas of consumerism, marketing ethics, and social responsibility will be made. There are many approaches to solving these issues. Among these approaches three stand out as likely courses of action. They are *increased regulation, better public information*, and *a broader marketing philosophy.*

The marketing manager's job is becoming more concerned with the total environment of the firm. As a consequence, the manager must make the effort to understand and work with the broader social context within which the firm operates.

PROGRAMMED REVIEW

1. The marketing department operates in an environment external to the firm. Events occurring in the environment are usually felt first by marketing personnel, who in turn interpret and transmit them to top management. It is ________________ that reacts to significant environmental changes. This is why it is argued that marketing generally mirrors changes in the entire business environment.

marketing

2. Relationships with the environment are called externalities. How the firm relates to these ________________ has a significant effect on the relative degree of success achieved by the firm.

externalities

3. Traditionally, society has encouraged ________________ to aid in providing a better life for people by providing ________________ possessions.

marketing
physical

4. Recently, an antimaterialist subculture has developed and is challenging the value of materialism. It is suggested that synthesis of the two value systems will occur. Currently, however, ________________ is the focus of much of this value conflict.

marketing

5. How marketing adapts to these conflicting issues will largely determine the ________________ that will emerge in our business system.

synthesis

6. A major problem in coping with the contemporary social issues emerging from this clash of values is the lack of evaluative standards. Without such ________________ it is difficult to agree on problems or solutions.

standards

7. For example, we lack a reliable index for the quality of life. There are measures for the quantities produced and sold; however, they do not indicate the ________________ of life.

quality

8. Today marketers are concerned with a variety of social issues. The three major categories of ________________ issues are consumerism, marketing ethics, and social responsibility.

social

9. ________________ is a protest against certain abuses and malpractices of individuals and firms within the marketing system.

consumerism

10. Some people have argued that the use of ________________ is proof that the marketing concept has failed. There are two reasons used to support this argument. One is that not enough ________________ have adopted the concept and the other is that the ________________ concept itself has not made firms responsive.

consumerism
firms
marketing

11. Another position is that consumerism provides marketers with new opportunities. Generally, ____________________ support the ____________________ philosophy.

marketers
consumerism

12. The authors of your text believe that the ____________________ concept will be expanded to include the tenets of consumerism.

marketing

13. Critics of the competitive marketing system cite six separate arguments against the system. The first criticism is that ____________________ costs are too high.

marketing

14. Your authors' reply is that the cost seems high only in relation to the production costs. Improved distribution methods have expanded the market for most products so that product ____________________ per unit have declined.

costs

15. Other ____________________ include that the marketing system is inefficient, that product quality and service are poor, that the marketing system has produced health hazards, that marketers engage in collusion and price fixing, and that consumers do not receive complete information.

criticisms

16. The answer to some of these charges is, "Yes, the criticism is valid." In other instances, the answer is, "Yes, but there are mitigating circumstances." In all cases, marketers are aware of the ____________________ and are interested in improving the conditions that led to them.

criticisms

17. An issue of serious concern to all involved is consumer rights. The clearest policy statement on consumer ____________________ was issued by the late President Kennedy. According to this statement, the consumer has the right to choose, to be heard, to be safeguarded, and to be informed.

rights

18. Five specific reactions are attributed to the consumer movement. They include passage of consumer legislation, additional consumer-protection agencies, the concept of class-action suits, the concept of mass-restitution suits, and ____________________ education.

consumer

19. Class-____________________ suits are brought by private citizens on behalf of any group of ____________________ for damages caused by unfair business practices.

action
consumers

20. Firms have responded positively to consumerism in several ways. Some firms have provided the means for ____________________ to have their grievances redressed.

consumers 21. Other firms have used advertising strategies that relate better to the consumer's real needs. Still other ______________________ hold executive-consumer discussions.

firms 22. Another approach aims to reduce ______________________ after-sale frustration. Firms have also established separate corporate departments to work on consumer issues.

consumer 23. There are three basic ethical philosophies presented as bases for marketing ethics The ______________________ philosophies are utilitarianism, moral idealism, and intuitionism.

ethical 24. These ethical ______________________ may be used to evaluate the ethics of a marketing act.

philosophies 25. Utilitarianism looks to the consequences of an ______________________ to assess its morality.

act 26. Moral ______________________ sets a general standard of conduct composed of specific rules. The act is then judged by these rules.

idealism 27. Intuitionism seeks to uncover the motives of the participants in the ______________________.

act 28. Individuals and organizations have standards of ethical behavior based on these ethical ______________________. Often there is a conflict between the individual's ethic and the organizational ethic.

philosophies 29. One method of coping with conflict of this nature is the development of and adherence to a professional ______________________.

ethic 30. A variety of ethical problems faces the marketer. For example, there are ______________________ questions concerning research, product management, channel strategy, pricing, and promotion.

ethical 31. Ethical problems concerning promotion involve personal selling and advertising. Of the two areas of ______________________, advertising problems are more often discussed.

promotion 32. Ethical concern in advertising includes the issue of advertising to children. The focus of the concern over such ______________________ is that it exerts an undue influence on children.

advertising 33. Social ______________________ is one of the broadest and most nebulous topics in marketing. Two basic issues in the area of social responsibility are (1) the relationship between social responsibility and the profit motive and (2) the locus for socially responsible decisions within the organization.

responsibility

34. Traditionally, management was responsible to customers, employees, and stockholders. Now the concept of ____________________ has been expanded to include the entire social framework.

responsibility

35. Many decisions that are not made by marketers ultimately become marketing problems because of the ____________________ department's relationship with the environment. For example, the decision to continue the operation of a profitable but air-polluting plant will be made by others, but marketing will probably be responsible for dealing with criticism from the community and other sources.

marketing

36. ____________________ responsibility is concerned not only with the decisions of an individual firm; it is also interested in the responsibility of the entire competitive marketing ____________________. The differences in marketing structures and products available to minority groups are examples of this problem.

social

system

37. Social ____________________ in marketing also includes concern for our environment via the concept of ecology.

responsibility

38. Specific ecology questions include planned obsolescence, environmental pollution, cultural ____________________, the recycling of waste materials, and the preservation of resources.

pollution

39. The resolution of the contemporary ____________________ issues of consumerism, social ____________________, and marketing ____________________ is extremely important.

social

responsibility

ethics

40. The three main approaches to solving these problems are increased regulation, better public information, and a more responsible ____________________ philosophy.

marketing

41. Increased ____________________ will probably occur. Consumers are, according to a recent survey, agreeable to the idea of more rules and regulations.

regulation

42. Better public ____________________ would help in resolving all the social issues discussed in this chapter. This would include improved labeling on packages.

information

43. An example of ____________________ information is unit pricing, which has been tried in some supermarkets. ____________________ pricing states all prices in terms of some recognized unit of measurement. By comparing unit prices of a commodity, the customer can readily determine which package is priced lower.

better unit concept

44. Broadening or furthering of the marketing concept is another possible approach to the resolution of contemporary social problems. To broaden the marketing ____________________ to include social responsibility, aggressive implementation is needed.

ASSIGNMENTS

1. Does the marketing manager of the following products and services have more responsibility to consumers or to nonconsumers? Why?
   (a) Little cigars
   (b) Wine
   (c) Children's toys
   (d) Rock concerts
   (e) Bank services
   (f) Radio stations
   (g) Off-track betting (legal)

   Would antimaterialists be against the expanded consumption of the goods and services listed?

2. To resolve the conflict between an individual's ethic and an organization's ethic, the development of a professional ethic together with a system of

enforcement was suggested in your text. Assume that a code of ethics and a method of indoctrination and enforcement will become a reality. List three advantages and three disadvantages for the consumer. Then list three advantages and three disadvantages for the marketing manager. (*Hint*: Doctors, lawyers, accountants, and others have codes and governing bodies with the power to sanction individual members.) Take your list to class and discuss.

3. Read every article concerned with consumerism in your local paper for one week. Write a summary of what you learned.

4. Make a list of the typical marketing externalities for each of the organizations listed below.

   (a) Hardware store

   (b) Full-service drug wholesaler

   (c) Manufacturer of ball bearings

   (d) Museum (city-owned)

CASELETS

1. Contemporary Social Issues in the Marketing of Agricultural Products

Ernie Fieldrow is a pretty happy guy. After ten years as the best apple picker in the Chiwawa Valley, he was able to save enough to buy an orchard of his own. Of course, Ernie owes the bank a few thousand dollars, but he has a fine twenty-five-acre orchard that should provide enough income to pay off the note in twenty years and enough income above living expenses to send his children to college.

Ernie's apple crop is sold by a cooperative that is owned and run by the orchardists in the Chiwawa Valley. He has been a very active coop member and was recently elected to the board of directors. At yesterday's meeting a disturbing issue was raised.

The first item on the agenda was a report by a team of marketing students from a local university. The students had researched the coop's advertising program that stressed the theme of *eat apples and keep healthy.* The report was technical and well-done. The students concluded, "We have found that the average consumer isn't motivated by the health-giving benefits of apples. He responds better to appeals that relate eating fresh apples to *the good life. . . .*" During the discussion period the students again stressed the appeal to hedonism and suggested that the coop change its advertising them to that indicated by their findings.

Board chairman Bill Massanbrunk was horrified at the thought. Bill specified that since apples were in fact good for a person's health, they should be sold as a health aid. He was not interested in the students' suggestion.

Lana Sack also disagreed with the theme suggested by the students because it was deceptive: eating an apple does not guarantee that the consumer will have *the good life.*

Errol Flunt thought the idea of encouraging hedonism was *cultural pollution* of the worst kind.

When everyone had commented, they turned to Ernie for his opinion. Ernie simply indicated that if the theme suggested by the students would help increase the consumption of fresh apples and efficiently remind people of the coop's brand, then he favored the change.

There was no response to his comment.

QUESTIONS

1. What is a deceptive advertising theme? Do you agree with Lana? with Errol?
2. What should the coop do about its advertising theme?
3. Is Ernie's suggestion socially responsible?

2. The Social Responsibility of Ovid Augraten

Ovid Augraten, owner-manager of Little P's Restaurant, has problems. For six years Mr. Augraten's place has been a favorite luncheon and dinner spot in an eastern town of five thousand people. Although the restaurant's decor is modest and its location is not the best, it has been successful because of a specialty item—a casserole.

Last week the student newspaper at the local university printed an editorial charging that Mr. Augraten's casserole does not contain the nutritional value necessary to meet the minimum requirement for a full meal. The following day the town newspaper contained an article that mentioned in passing that certain ingredients in Mr. Augraten's casserole were harvested by nonunion workers. Then, while being interviewed by a local newscaster, Mr. Augraten commented that some ingredients in the casserole were imported. The newscaster was shocked.

Since then Mr. Augraten's life has been one headache after another. The student senate at the local university has passed a resolution denouncing his lack of responsibility to his customers and the community for not providing a meal that meets the nutritional standard. He has received letters and phone calls from irate individuals. In addition, a local action group has petitioned the town council to take away his license to do business because he did not use union ingredients. From time to time, pickets representing various interest groups have appeared in front of his restaurant.

In spite of all this, business has slowed very little. From informal discussions with regular customers, including a good number of students, Mr. Augraten has concluded that very few of his customers are upset with him.

QUESTIONS

1. Specifically, what are Mr. Augraten's responsibilities to society, to his customers, to his community, to nonconsumers of his service, to his family, and to his employees?
2. What would you recommend Mr. Augraten do in this case?